ALAN,

ENJOY.

# HIGH PERFORMANCE COACHING

## "The New Science of Performance"

*America's Most Trusted Coach*

The 3-Step Solution to
Immediately Take Charge
and Transform Your Mental,
Emotional, Physical and
Financial Future

## STEVEN GRIFFITH

# PRAISE FOR
# HIGH PERFORMANCE COACHING

"Steven's High Performance Coaching has had a profound impact on my ability to coach, present, sell, and truly connect with my clients. Because of his coaching and tools, I was able to quickly take my business to the next level. I recommend his program to any professional who wants to get fast results and rapidly grow their business."

> — Mark MacDonald, *Author of the New York Times Bestsellers* Body Confidence *and* Why Kids Make You Fat, *Founder & CEO, Venice Nutrition, a featured fitness & nutrition expert for Dr. OZ, CNN, Access Hollywood, Chelsea Lately*

"All successful top achievers have coaches and are action-oriented. That's why they are top achievers! **If you're ready to break through barriers** that you may not even realize are mentally holding you back from achieving your highest performance, **then you need to coach with Steven right away. Not only does he produce results, but he comes from an authentic place of truly caring about serving and making a positive difference!**"

> — James Malinchak, *Featured on ABC's Hit TV Show, "Secret Millionaire," Co-Author,* Chicken Soup for the College Soul, *Founder, www.BigMoneySpeaker.com*

"I have known Steven for almost 20 years. When it comes to coaching and performance, **his expertise can provide you with the guidance to successfully achieve your goals.**"

> — Eric Karros, *Former Los Angeles Dodger star, Fox TV Sports Commentator*

"Your method of coaching has given me the results I have been looking for over 20 years. **Working with you, I finally am free from struggling with limiting beliefs.** I feel I am a different person—stronger, happier, at peace. **My relationships with my family and friends have improved; I am more effective at work, and have greater insight into all my work and personal relationships; I am more open, expressive, and confident.** I can't wait to see how my life continues to shift and open up to the world of possibilities."

— **Gina Anastasia,** *Chief People Officer, UberMedia and former COO at Rent.com*


"Over the years, I have had many coaches and **Steven is one that is truly gifted at helping individuals be the best they can be.** As a professional athlete, I knew I needed to do everything I could to have the competitive edge and that is why I hired Steven. He is a true professional who has dedicated his career to helping individuals from sports to the business world get results—**If you want the edge, I recommend his coaching.**"

— **Tyus Edney,** *Director of Basketball Operations UCLA and Former NBA and Euroleague basketball star*


"In my career, I have had the honor to spend time with many successful people. They all possess amazing qualities that contribute to their success. Steven coaches people in those qualities. **He has the ability to guide people to break through their own barriers in performance and communication.** He has helped me tremendously over the years to be mindful, stay focused, communicate effectively, and professionally flourish."

— **Doug DeLuca,** *Executive Producer of ABC Television's "Jimmy Kimmel Live"*

"Steven, your Coaching program is extremely powerful and effective. **Through your guidance, I have grown in my ability to communicate and deal with individuals effectively as a coach, leader, manager, and problem solver.** Thanks for your help. I highly encourage anyone looking to improve who they are and increase their chances of success to take the time and learn from you."

> — **Tim Adams,** *LA KINGS Head Strength and Conditioning Coach and former Los Angeles Raiders Coach*

"With Steven, I've got a genuine guy in my corner rooting, supporting, and guiding me towards my awareness of greater abundance and joy on all levels, both personally and professionally. Steven provides a supportive, fresh perspective that I appreciate greatly. His approach is very holistic, which has opened my mind and heart to more deeply connect with the wealth of strength I **am allowing myself to more deeply achieve and receive in my life.**"

> — **Nick Segal,** *Founder/President, Partner's Trust*

"I was having great success in growing my business, but was working myself into the ground and felt my health was deteriorating. I knew my work/life balance was completely off. Steven quickly helped me get on track and in balance — working smarter with more ease all while growing my business. If you want a trusted advisor in your corner who will help you get to the next level, Steven is the Coach for you."

> —**Pat Norton,** *ISN Premier Founder, Managing Partner*

"After helping me through a very important corporate negotiation, I have found Steven's coaching to be of great value in real-world applications. **His insights and recommendations helped me to stay calm, focused, and relaxed through the whole communication/ negotiation process,** which yielded me a very successful contract."

> — **Dr. George Kosmides,** *Founder, DrKosmides.com*

"When I started working with Steven, I knew what I wanted to accomplish, I just didn't know how to get there on my own. Thanks to Steven's tailor-made coaching program, I was able to implement his techniques in order to reach my goal of starting my own consulting business. Within two weeks, I had two clients and was standing on the precipice of more business than I could handle on my own. Steven Griffith is the real deal. He makes dreams come true."

> — **Mike Montgomery,** *Montlake Group,*
> *Business and Political Consultant*

"I have always been passionate about my business in helping people become financially free. I knew I wanted to help even more people — which meant getting better at selling. Steven's system changed my mindset to one of serving and his step-by-step system has helped me be more compassionate and confident in the sales process and handle any objections, which has led me to enroll more clients into my program then ever! If you want a system that makes selling easy, I recommend Steven's program."

> — **David Phelps,** *Founder, Freedom Founders*

"In a world of increasingly confusing roles between men and women, communication and relationships themselves are suffering. Steven is that rare individual who understands the brain and the biological differences between the sexes. He is an expert at coaching both women and men to effectively communicate so they can understand each other and have positive relationships that flourish."

> — **Dr. Pat Allen,** *Author,* Getting to I Do *and Founder,*
> *the WANT Institute*

"Working with Steven Griffith has made a profound difference in both my professional and personal life. His unique abilities to detect root challenges helped me identify barriers that held me back and coached me in a supportive manner for me to take action outside my comfort zone. He gave me the tools that instantly created new strategies to overcome my old challenges. With his coaching, he helped me understand issues from a different perspective enabling me to become a better communicator, negotiator, and listener. Because of this, my relationships have been greatly enhanced with both clients and colleagues."

— **Maria Gobic Javas,** *National Leasing Manager, National Promotions and Advertising*

"I was looking for a competitive edge to take my game to the next level and grow my business. When I found Steven, it was more than I expected. He has helped me see areas where I was being held back that I didn't even know were there. I now have a business plan that overlaps into a life plan. He has been an advocate for my success in every area of my life. The results have been tremendous!"

— **Grant Heller,** *Principle, Pioneer Wealth Partners*

"If you are committed to your own excellence in life, then look no further than Steven Griffith and his High Performance Process. He helped pull me out of a huge hole that I found myself in a few years back. Not only did he help pull me out, but he also created a blueprint for me to launch forward at a rate that I did not think was possible. I cannot recommend his process enough! There are only a few people out there who truly operate at this level and Steven is one of them."

— **John Dewey,** *Founder, JohnDewey.com and Prosperitage.com*

"As an independent real estate investor/entrepreneur I wanted to have somebody on my team who could help me accelerate my success. I was doing well in my business and knew I had more potential but needed a clearer path to become more efficient, effective, and profitable. Steven in our first session identified my blind spot (What was holding me back) and things immediately started shifting in a positive direction. I am more calm, efficient, and balanced. Steven has built my confidence up to an all-time high and I now have the right tools for creating success in my business and in my life."

— **Adam Barshay,** *Founding Principal, Anacapa Realty Investments*

"If you want to make immediate and positive changes in yourself and you are looking for a life-changing experience, look no further. Steven has helped me to discover what is truly important to me and help me see and shift the things that I didn't even know were holding me back! I now see for the first time what my true passion and purpose is in life. If you are on a mission to create a fulfilling and purpose-driven life, work with Steven."

— **Lorrie M. Ross,** *National Buyer Nordstrom*

"Steven Griffith's High Performance Coaching is by far the best investment I have made for my business. As an artist, I have always been uncomfortable with the selling and negotiating process. **Not any more – Steven successfully walked me through the biggest negotiations of my career and helped me close my first six-figure commissioned project!** Steven has taught me that I can be both a great artist and run a successful and profitable business. I now have the exact blueprint for success. I truly appreciate his integrity and priceless expertise. STEVEN ROCKS!!"

— **Kristie Fujiyama Kosmides,** *Artist, www.kfkart.com*

"Steven Griffith is the most effective business coach I have had the opportunity of working with. **Utilizing just one of his many techniques helped my business grow in a down market.** Anyone considering hiring Steven will find that he is an immediate asset!"

— **George Felactu,** *President, ML Consulting*

"Steven is a great coach who has helped me get through my BS (Blind Spots). He has held me to be accountable to myself in what I want out of life. Since working with Steven, I have a trusted advisor to help in both critical business and personal decisions. Since working with him, I am happier, more self-aware, and healthier."

—**Pete Zachary,** *Founder, NPA*

"**Steven has been critical to my personal and professional growth.** Inherently being a shy and introverted person, Steven has taught me valuable communication skills that have allowed me to speak dynamically in front of large groups of people. As well, my ability to handle high-pressure sales situations has grown tremendously. **I highly recommend Steven for anyone looking to take their game to the next level!**"

— **Mike Hibner,** *Director of Key Accounts, Star Trac*

"As a veteran of the real estate game for over 33 years and selling over 3.4 billion dollars in real estate, I've seen it all. Steven Griffith is truly one of the best at getting your Mindset focused and taking action on the things that are going to make you money NOW!"

—**Charles Pence,** *Founder, Partner's Trust*

"Every interaction is the most important. This includes those with my clients, partners, colleagues, competitors, family, and friends. Griffith's system has given me the power to build trust and rapport immediately, aligning myself to the highest level of confidence completely transforming my conversations. **And most importantly, he has given me that slight edge, which has made a huge impact in competing for and closing business.**"

— David Sullivan, *VP of Sales, CCC, Inc.*

"I first hired Steven 3 years ago for help with my career. However, what I have experienced and learned was such more than I could ever imagined. His wisdom and knowledge are so powerful and vast both for business and personally. Whether you are looking at what to do next in a career, a relationship OR just wanting to be the best version of yourself, Steven is the guy to get you there! Thank you for all of your guidance, Steven. I would not be where I am without you."

—Chris Campbell, *Vice President of Production, Shine America*

"**Steven Griffith's Coaching program is an easy, systematic approach to getting results.** It has helped us company-wide to effectively communicate, service our customers, and empower our employees with tools that work. I highly recommend it."

— Jim McKenzie, *COO, NASM*
*(National Academy of Sports Medicine)*

"Steven proved to be an invaluable resource in my life. **He was the only person who was able to target, identify, and crystallize stumbling blocks from my past and guide me through to a more successful, brighter chapter in my life** in a very short amount of time."

— Geoff Silverman, *Literary, TV & Film Manager, Rain Management, Santa Monica, CA*

# HIGH PERFORMANCE COACHING

## "The New Science of Performance"

The 3-Step Solution to Immediately Take Charge and Transform Your Mental, Emotional, Physical and Financial Future

## STEVEN GRIFFITH

### EDITED BY DAVID CHRISTEL

STEVEN GRIFFITH
HIGH PERFORMANCE COACHING

*High Performance Coaching*
*xiii*

Title: *High Performance Coaching*
Subtitle: *The 3-Step Solution to Immediately Take Charge and Transform Your Mental, Emotional, Physical and Financial Future*
Author: Steven Griffith
Published by: Steven Griffith & Associates
www.StevenGriffith.com

Cover and interior design: Dawn Teagarden
Front cover photograph: Armen Asadorian
Front jacket flap and back cover photography: Chris Harvey
Interior graphics: Dawn Teagarden and Nakayama Hideaki

ISBN: 978-0-615-61144-0

High Performance Coaching

310-575-0101
www.StevenGriffith.com

Tom and I in Chicago

*To my longtime friend and boxing coach, Tom Delaney —
you taught me through your kindness and compassion how
to be a great coach. It is to you I dedicate this book.*

# Acknowledgements

I want to acknowledge all the coaches and mentors I have had over the years — I have learned something from every one of you, as well as the thousands of clients and students with whom I have been so blessed to work. It would be impossible to thank everyone who has had a positive impact on my life and career, so please forgive me if I've not included you in these acknowledgments as that is not my intention.

Thank you to my friend and boxing coach, Tom Delaney, for your kindness and compassion, and your model of how to be an awesome coach — I carry that with me every day. Mom: for all your sacrifices you made all along the way for me. To Gary De Rodriguez: you started me on the path of helping me find my true self. Marilyn Youngbird, thank you for one of the most transformational experiences in my first vision quest to help me see my true path.

My friend John Dewey for your continuous support on this journey, many hours of life discussions, and your interviewing me for this book. Mark McDonald, the world's best nutritionist: Your friendship, inspiration, and trust in letting me work with many of your clients in the early days and your educating me on nutrition has been the fuel for my body to work. My friends Kristie, George, and Sophia Kosmides for your constant love and support. David Christel, for your continuing support in friendship, fine writing skills on this book, and flannel wardrobe. My friend John Carnes for your constant encouragement, enthusiasm, support, and friendship. Dr.

Pat Allen: Your teaching, training, support, and wisdom in human relationships/communication have been life-changing for me and every person I coach. Dr. Linda Steele: Thank you for your loving spirit, support, and encouragement of my work. John Morrow for your support and friendship all these years. Dawn, for doing a great job on the formatting and cover for this book. James Malinchak, for coaching, inspiring, and motivating me to get my message out and this book into the world.

Jon Kabat-Zinn, Joan Halifax, Eckhart Tolle: You have all had a great impact on mindfulness in my personal life, as well as my coaching philosophy. Dr. Dan Siegel for your teaching about the brain, communication, and relationships. David Rock for your work on the brain and performance. C.J. Matthews for your ongoing friendship and support. Rivka for helping me tell and craft my story. Geoffrey White, for your friendship and guidance in difficult times and always helping me see the path. Charmain Page: Thank you for your love, wisdom, and firm push every time I needed it.

Yuki for your deep love, support, and seeing me for who I really am. Allen Hoey for your friendship all these years and your sage wisdom. Armen Asadorian for your great photography. Chris Harvey for your creative influence, support, friendship, and your masterful photography. Thom Knoles for your wisdom and guidance. And John Wooden, your model as a coach and your Pyramid of Success have been a great inspiration to me and my work.

# WELCOME TO HIGH PERFORMANCE COACHING!

## The New Science of Performance™

**Have you stalled out, hit the wall, or leveled off in your career, finances, health, or relationships?**

### Are you experiencing...

- High stress, energy, weight, sleep, or health issues?

- Inefficient and ineffective time management?

- A lack of purpose in your life?

- Distractions and a lack of focus?

- Challenges with your financial situation?

- Difficult personal or business communications?

- Feeling alone or unsupported in your business or life?

- A lack of balance in your life?

- Feeling stuck and not accelerating in your business or career?

- A lack of motivation?

**High Performance Coaching** is the New Science of Performance. It's not therapy or life coaching, but a performance system that bridges the gap from your potential and what's holding you back to your own personal High Performance. This system creates fast, measurable, real-world results — not just some textbook ideas. What this means to you is living a High Performance life right Now!

If you're not performing at your highest level, it's not your fault — and here's why. What most people don't realize is that they are missing out on their true potential because of Blind Spots that they don't even know they have when it comes to career, finances, relationships, and health. Blind Spots cause people to underperform in business, have unsatisfying personal relationships, have difficulty communicating with people, experience high stress, feel they're not advancing in their career, not making enough money, experiencing poor health, or to simply check out from living their life's purpose — all due to simple belief patterns, misaligned values, and ineffective communication strategies that are holding them back because they can't see them and therefore can't change them. That's why they're underperforming. The High Performance Coaching System brings you the latest science-based tools in a new, cutting-edge systematic approach for you to have a break through to your next-level results.

> ## "All top performers do it themselves, but never alone."
> — Steven Griffith

Imagine having one of America's most trusted High Performance Coaches at your side who has a proven track record working with large and small organizations and with the world's top Business Executives, CEOs, Entrepreneurs, Professional and Olympic Athletes, and Entertainment Professionals and Celebrities. With my expert system, I will help you navigate anything that comes your way so you will feel confident, in control of your future, and get the results you want in business and in life!

*"Give me 5 minutes and I can uncover the Blind Spot that is holding you back from your ultimate success."*

My System is designed to be a fast, 3-Step process.

1. I identify your Blind Spot related to **old** limiting beliefs, negative emotions, high stress, and poor performance.

2. We neutralize your Blind Spot and your old limiting **BELIEFS** and create **NEW STRATEGIES** and resources that are aligned with the **VALUES, PURPOSE,** and **GOALS** you truly want in life.

3. I coach you on your individual High Performance and **COMMUNICATION** strategies for ongoing permanent results and High Performance in your business and personal life.

The High Performance Pyramid

**When your beliefs, values, life purpose, and communication are aligned, the following results allow you to perform at your highest level:**

- Increased freedom

- Increased focus

- Decreased stress

- Emotional balance

- Increased productivity

- Increased income

- Mindful living

- Fulfilled life purpose

- Increased health and wellness

- More time

- A balanced life

- Quality relationships

"Make every day a masterpiece."
— John Wooden, Legendary UCLA Basketball Coach

# SOME OF STEVEN'S CEO, ENTREPRENEUR, EXECUTIVE, ATHLETIC, AND ENTERTAINMENT CLIENTS

**Mark MacDonald** – Author of the New York Times Bestsellers *Body Confidence* and *Why Kids Make You Fat,* Founder & CEO, Venice Nutrition, a featured fitness & nutrition expert for Dr. OZ, CNN, Access Hollywood, Chelsea Lately

**Gina Anastasia** – Chief People Officer, UberMedia Former COO at Rent.com

**Steve Sarkisian** – Head Football Coach, USC

**Mike Piazza** – MLB Catcher, Future Baseball Hall of Famer

**Pete Zachary** – Founder, NPA

**Doug DeLuca** – Executive Producer, ABC Television's "Jimmy Kimmel Live"

**Mike Montgomery** – Montlake Group, Business and Political Consultant

**George Roumain** – USA Olympic Volleyball Medalist

**Mike Hibner** – Director of Key Accounts, Star Trac

**David Sullivan** – Senior VP of Sales, CCC, Inc.

**Nomar Garciaparra** – All Star MLB Player

**Don MacLean** – NBA Player, Fox TV Commentator

**Dr. Linda Steele** – Psychologist/Drug intervention specialist

**Charlie McPhee** – Sr. VP, Public Storage

**Tim Adams** – Former LA Kings Strength & Conditioning Coach and LA Raiders Coach

**Dr. George Kosmides** – Founder, DrKosmides.com

**Tyus Edney** – Director of Basketball Operations UCLA and Former NBA and Euroleague Basketball Star

**Mike Sherrard** – 3-Time NFL Super Bowl Player

**Geoff Silverman** – Literary, TV & Film Manager, Rain Producer Management

**Dave Olear** – VP, Wells Fargo

**Eric Karros** – Former Los Angeles Dodger Star and Fox TV Sports Commentator

**Charles Pence** – Realtor, Founder, Partner's Trust

**Maria Gobic Javas** – National Leasing Manager National Promotions and Advertising

**Kristy Morrell** – RD, Head Athletic Dietitian, University of Southern California

**Chad Lewis** – NFL Pro Bowler

**Luis De Fretiz** – Former Mr. Universe and World-Class Fitness Expert/Coach

**Jim McKenzie** – COO, NASM (National Academy of Sports Medicine)

**David Phelps** – Founder, Freedom Founders

**Pat Norton** – ISN Premier Founder, Managing Partner

**Nick Segal** – Founder/President, Partner's Trust

**Gunnar Munson** – Founder and CEO, Sasquatch Coffee and The Bigfoot Research Institute

**Chris Campbell** – Vice President of Production, Shine America

**Eric Hutchings** – Founder and COO, Compliance Medical Services

**George Felactu** – High Performance Sports Trainer, President, ML Consulting

**Jason Kendall** – All Star MLB player

**Rob Fredrickson** – NFL player

**Adam Barshay** – Founding Principal, Anacapa Realty Investments

## Organizations

Wells Fargo

University of Southern California

Pepperdine University

UCLA

NPA

National Academy of Sports Medicine

Citibank

MonaVie

ADP

Coldwell Banker

Los Angeles Police Department

Venice Nutrition

United States Bankcard Services

Members of the MLB, NFL, NBA, and NHL

Partner's Trust

ISN Premier

Jimmy Kimmel Live

# HIGH PERFORMANCE COACHING

## "The New Science of Performance"

The 3-Step Solution to Immediately Take Charge and Transform Your Mental, Emotional, Physical and Financial Future

## STEVEN GRIFFITH

### EDITED BY DAVID CHRISTEL

# Table of Contents

# INTRODUCTION

*"You have to expect things of yourself*
*before you can do them."*

— Michael Jordan, NBA Hall of Famer

Welcome to the HPC 3-Step System. If you are reading this book, it is not by accident: You are ready for a breakthrough. If you have been struggling, have become stuck, leveled off or hit the wall in your career, finances, relationships or health and know you inherently have more potential than you're utilizing, then you are ready for a breakthrough.

So what exactly is a breakthrough?

Break·through (Google definition)

1. A sudden, dramatic, and important discovery or development.

2. An instance of achieving success in a particular sphere or activity.

My personal definition is:

> "A breakthrough is a moment in time when you become free from what has been holding you back."
> — Steven Griffith

We have all had them if we look back at our lives — a place that you may have struggled (a bad relationship, dead end job, poor health, etc.), you made a decision, took action, and you changed it.

It may have gone on for days, months or years, but in a moment, you made a decision you could no longer tolerate the circumstances — you took action and became free from it.

Our breakthroughs are either acts of desperation (we can't take it anymore) or inspiration (someone or something inspired us to be a better version of ourselves).

It breaks my heart to see people struggling and not living their heart's desire. That's why I have dedicated my whole life to help people have breakthroughs. My mission for over 25 years has been to bring the best tools and strategies for people to break through the limitations of their past to have what they truly desire in business and in life! I wrote this book to bring my one-on-one coaching and seminar work to as many people as I can so they can be free to choose a life unrestricted from their pasts. A new breakthrough is waiting for you right now!

A High Performance breakthrough is not complicated or even difficult. You are ready, the time is now. It doesn't matter if you have just started out in business or are a veteran, a novice or expert in your field, young or old. You just need the right mindset, skillset, and the right formula. It requires new patterns of thought, actions, and strategies. That's what the HPC System is all about.

What most people do is try harder to get unstuck — it's not about trying harder. Many times, the past will trick you into using the same strategies and thinking, which will yield little or no results. The logic of "trying harder" is enticing, seductive, and it rarely works. The rules have changed. You can't do the same thing expecting a different result. It's the *right* effort, not *more* effort. High Performance breakthroughs are available to you!

It's time for a new game. The HPC System will help you leverage up your results in less time, more efficiently, and with greater ease.

Whether it's career or business advancement, better relationships, more income, better health and wellness, more fun, or you just want to be happy, find your true purpose, and get your life back in balance. This System is your opportunity to do just that.

We, by the very nature of who we are biologically and spiritually, are designed to be the best we can. The "law of nature" dictates that all things in nature fundamentally must express their full design — so must you!

Just as when an acorn is planted, it has one intention and one intention only: to grow into a tree as big and strong as it can with as many branches and leaves as possible. In the right environment, it will flourish and do just that.

Wallace Wattles, one of the original experts on personal development, wealth and prosperity, in his 1910 book *The Science of Getting Rich*, says this about our inherent design and the desire to be the best we can be: "The desire for increase is inherent in all nature; it is the fundamental impulse of the universe.... Every living thing is under this necessity for continuous advancement; where increase of life ceases, dissolution and death set in at once."

The Impression of Increase is a key to your success and is based on the concepts of prosperity, abundance, and increase. Wattles further states, "To make every act and thought constructive, everyone must convey the idea of increase. Steadily hold in mind the thought of advancement for yourself; know that you are advancing toward what you want, and act and speak in this faith. Then every word and act will convey the idea of advancement and increase to others, and they will be drawn to you. Always remember that what all people are seeking for is increase."

What this means to you is all human activities are based on the desire of increase, to be the best we can be and have the best we can have: love, home, beauty, luxury, knowledge, health, wealth, and wellbeing. If you're not doing this, you're actually going against your inherent nature.

Many times with clients, I've dealt with this Someday Syndrome: "When (this happens) _____, then I will _____."

- When I balance my life, I can be healthy and fit.
- When I save some money, then I will go back to school.
- When I lose 20 pounds, then I can have the relationship of my dreams.
- When my kids turn 18, then I can start living my life again.
- When I get my MBA, then I'll be smart enough to advance in my career.
- When the economy changes, then I'm going to be successful.
- When I own a house, then I will have made it.
- When…when…when….

You have to start with the mindset of "How I can" vs. "Why I can't."

You have to first make a decision that you want something with full conviction, which then forces your mind to find the way. It NEVER happens in reverse. That's why people stay stuck. To change, we must seek information, knowledge, wisdom, coaching, etc. to become a successful, High Performing person. Einstein said that, "We can't solve problems by using the same kind of thinking we used to create them."

Wattles had it 100 percent right except for one thing: to will yourself into the Impression of Increase and the next-level of performance in today's high-paced, competitive world is nearly impossible when you're operating in a Blind Spot.

Blind Spots are created from negative subconscious conditioning from our past, which creates a misalignment with our beliefs, values, communication, and our life purposes causing ineffective actions and strategies that keep us underperforming in our careers, finances, relationships, and health and wellness.

I've learned in my years of coaching people just like you — entrepreneurs, business owners, CEOs, executives, athletes, celebrities, and entertainment professionals — that there are "hidden roadblocks" keeping you stuck and struggling and they are Blind Spots!

If you're not performing at your highest level, it's not your fault. It's because of a Blind Spot that you don't even know you have.

Most people have been misled because of this. They believe that if you set a goal, you just start working towards it, just stay motivated, and it will happen. Not if you're in a Blind Spot.

When people don't reach their goals, they feel like something is wrong with them, they just do not deserve them, or just have bad luck. They become tired and fatigued doing the same thing over and over never realizing that they're in a Blind Spot. They become demoralized or just plain quit.

I've seen this cycle over and over. That's why I created the HPC 3-Step System to help you identify your Blind Spots in order to align your beliefs, values, purpose, and goals so you can perform at your highest level and have the life you want.

The truth is that most people are focusing in the wrong place. The right place to focus is by identifying and breaking through your Blind Spot. You can then focus on what is the most important aspect of getting to the next level, which is WHO YOU NEED TO BE TO HAVE WHAT YOU WANT. It is nearly impossible to be who you need to be when you are in your Blind Spot. As you'll learn in this book, you can't change what you can't see. I will take you through a process in Chapter 4 that will quickly identify who you need to be and what your Blind Spot is that's shielding you from your High Performance and your next-level results.

My motto has been for a long time: *"Give me 5 minutes and I can uncover the Blind Spot that is holding you back from your ultimate success."* After working with thousands of people just like you for over 20 years, I've created the ability to quickly see an individual's Blind Spot within five minutes and that's what you'll learn to do with this High Performance System, as well as uncover your true values, beliefs, purpose, and goals.

You have to want to break through to your next level bad enough, and I know you do, that's why you're reading this book. It's all possible and within your reach. It's time for you to uplevel your game, uplevel your mindset, uplevel your skillset, and uplevel your income and your impact on the world.

> "The very best thing you can do for the whole world is to make the most of yourself."
> — Wallace Wattles

A High Performer is a person who:

1. knows what their life's purpose is,

2. has beliefs, values, and goals aligned with their purpose,

3. can sustain focused energy and effort to reach goals in the face of failures and setbacks while remaining optimistic,

4. has the ability to consistently regulate thoughts and emotions that work *for* them rather than *against* them,

5. responds to the world in a rational way rather than in a reactive, emotional way,

6. knows that happiness is based not on what happens, but how they interpret what happens,

7. doesn't take things personally,

8. lives in a mindfulness way (present in the moment),

9. doesn't compare themselves or their situation to others, and

10. doesn't whine, complain or make excuses, and takes 100 percent responsibility for their performance in business and in life.

Have you ever:

- felt there's not enough time in the day?

- felt unfocused and distracted?

- felt you're not accelerating in your business or career?

- felt unbalanced in work and life?

- set a goal and not achieved it?

- been so stressed out that you are just trying to get through the day?

- been in an unfulfilling relationship?

- tried endlessly to get in shape and lose that 10, 15, 20, or more pounds?

- worked hard, but are still not where you want to be financially?

- felt like your life has no purpose?

- felt like you're not having enough fun?

The HPC 3-Step System is for you if you are striving to have a better life. Like you, most of my clients are already successful and desire to be the best they can. You may have had traction, have become stuck or plateaued in your business, career, or life and want to get to the next level. Even if you feel like you've already done everything you can or think you've reached as high as you can, the High Performance System will help you achieve more than you have before.

This book will show you how to:

- have more happiness, freedom, and time,

- advance your business and career,

- have more energy and less stress,

- uncover your Blind Spot and limiting beliefs that are holding you back,

- increase your income,

- have more healthy relationships,

- communicate more effectively,

- live mindfully,

- increase your business results,

- uncover your true purpose,

- stop, start, or change behaviors that are not getting you positive results,

- rationally respond versus react emotionally,

- set goals and get them fast,

- improve your health and wellness, and

- get unstuck.

After working with and being a trusted advisor, coach, and advocate to some of the most successful leaders, entrepreneurs, executives, CEOs, business owners, professional athletes, entertainment professionals and coaches in the world, I have simplified the top research and methods into an easy-to-use, science-based, real-world program to get you fast results — the New Science of Performance.

Within these pages, you will see the simple instructions that create massive results. So if you are ready to immediately take charge and transform your life, you have this book not by chance, but because you are ready for a breakthrough to get the results you've always wanted — NOW!

# Chapter 1

# THE BEGINNING OF HIGH PERFORMANCE

*"Create your future from your future, not your past."*

— Werner Erhard, Founder of EST training and the Landmark Forum

# My Story

From my early upbringing, I never thought I would be a performance coach. I was born and raised in Chicago and the early days were not easy. My mom raised me and my younger brother. We were on and off food stamps and housing support. We lived in difficult times and my mom did the best she could.

I knew from an early age that I wanted a better life for me and my family, and the only way I saw out was through sports: football and later boxing. The problem was I didn't know how to change our environment and I felt like we were imprisoned. I could not escape the past. The past seemed to repeat itself day after day after day. Constant negative thoughts and emotions consumed me, and I lacked the skills to effectively turn them around.

I believed the only way out was sports because I was constantly hearing from my teachers over and over that I was a bad kid and not smart. Later, I found out as an adult that I have a light form of dyslexia that makes spelling, math, and some other areas of learning very challenging for me.

I can remember like yesterday being in the 3rd grade and having my gym teacher grab me by my ear, berate me, and pull me down the hallway. He was telling me "You're a bad kid, always getting in trouble, you're a loser." All because I'd said that I hadn't done something, but he believed I had. He insisted that, "You're responsible," and I kept insisting I wasn't. This had all happened before. I was constantly being singled out as "the bad kid" mainly because I was always arguing my point of view. Therefore, I got more than my share of "being in trouble." No matter what I said or did, I was labeled as a troublemaker.

I remember feeling different and powerless. My mom was divorced and back then, not many kids had divorced parents. For me, I felt completely alone and defenseless not having a dad. I believed that if nobody was going to protect me, then I needed to "bring it." With a deep sense of shame, I began believing what my environment appeared to be signaling me, that "I'm not smart, I'm bad, I'm a loser." I became very insensitive, guarded, and defensive. Over time, I went all the way over to the other extreme. I only had one direction to go and that was to get tougher. I began living the label "troublemaker" and "troubled kid."

So, I played several sports in high school: football, basketball, and baseball. I was a pretty good athlete — aggressive — but I was so tall and skinny, I was called "The giraffe." To overcome this, I made a decision to get bigger, faster, and stronger. So, I read all the books I could get my hands on. I talked to whomever I thought had coaching and tools for me to learn from. After graduation from high school, I also started boxing to help improve my football. What I did was train hard, built up my body, and two and a half years after graduating high school, I ended up on the top football recruiting lists for Junior College players. By then, I stood 6'5" and weighed about 230 pounds — that was up from my senior year in high school when I was just 6'3" and 180 pounds.

Jump forward to my second season Junior College game. It was mid-October in Chicago and I could smell success in the air. I was very excited as we were playing a home game to a sold out crowd, and a half a dozen football scouts sat in the stands that day to see me and a few other players.

It was the first quarter and my adrenalin was pumping. I took a deep breath, leaned forward in the huddle, and my play was called. I ran my pass route down the field, turned to catch the ball, and "BANG!"

I felt like I had just been shot! I found myself lying face down on the field with the smell of grass in my face and searing, lightning hot pain shooting down the back of my right leg — I had just torn my hamstring. In a flash, I felt all my dreams shatter.

The trainers helped me to the sideline. I could barely focus my eyes because the pain was so intense. It was no longer contained to my leg, but filled my entire body.

When I got to the sideline, I glimpsed to my left and saw three middle-aged guys all looking down and writing in their scout books. It felt like they were signing the death certificate on my athletic career.

The next day, I immediately began rehab and about six weeks later, the trainer said "'Griff, we think you can play next week." We were in the "Like Cola Bowl" game for Junior Colleges (they had Junior College bowl games back then). So, they taped me from waist to calf, keeping my leg slightly bent so I could not fully extend it and injure myself any further. I got through the game and received a Division I scholarship at the end of the season.

Over the next three seasons, my leg would never be the same. Always in the back of my mind was, *"Will my hamstring hold up, will I tear it again today?"* I felt so vulnerable, frustrated, and angry taking the field each time and competing knowing I wasn't 100 percent, but at the same time, I couldn't let my dream go. All I knew was that I was nothing without football. As much as I tried to get back to my healthy self and hoped and prayed and trained, I was never the same. And, in the next three years, I tore my hamstring two more times!

After the third tear, I was completely devastated. The physical pain, although intense, paled in comparison to the mental anguish and torture I was in because all I believed I knew was sports. I was so angry that my body was letting me down. I felt there were no other options. I was committed to be a professional athlete, to become the professional athlete that I'd always dreamed of being.

So, I decided to pursue my professional boxing career instead. I had some early boxing successes being a two-time Golden Gloves finalist, once in the Chicago Golden Gloves and again in the Springfield Golden Gloves, and winning the Illinois State Heavyweight Boxing Championship. I moved to Los Angeles from Chicago and started training at the Broadway Boxing Gym in South Central Los Angeles with top pros including Tyrrell Biggs, the 1984 Olympic heavyweight Gold medalist. He had recently suffered a loss to Mike Tyson, something everyone did back then.

Things were going well. I was getting into great boxing shape, advancing my skills, and gaining some notoriety for my intense concentration and power — until one sparring session. I felt a pop in my back. It was a severely herniated disk. Eight months later, I had back surgery and my dreams of becoming a professional athlete were over. Four injuries in six years. I was crushed. Again, another injury, but this time it was the final blow! Lost, angry, frustrated and depressed, I didn't know what to do.

I was in complete turmoil. I still could only see myself in the world of sports. There were no other possibilities, nothing, because I only knew how to get bigger, stronger, faster, more powerful. My entire focus was about being an athlete.

After a period of frustration and anger, which I took out on the world around me, I realized that I had a BS in Exercise Science and wasn't capitalizing on it. I had previously worked as a trainer, so with a business partner, I opened one of the first privately run specialized sports training facilities in the United States called "The Yard." It was a center for peak athletic performance, located in Southern California. It has been home to current and former Major League sports legends and baseball All-Stars including Mike Piazza of the NY Mets, Jason Kendall of the Pittsburgh Pirates, Nomar Garciaparra of the Boston Red Sox, and LA Dodgers star, Eric Karros; NBA/Euroleague and UCLA star Tyus Edney; NFL Football Hall of Famer Andre Reed and quarterbacks Carson Palmer, Matt Leinart, and Tom Brady; Steve Sarkisian, former BYU quarterback and current USC head football coach; the 2014 Seattle Seahawks' Super Bowl champions, offensive team; and a host of professional and Olympic champions from virtually every sport.

With all these superstars coming to us, we immediately had great success. I had a beachfront condo, a sports car, and a gold Rolex. I was living large.

But, in spite of my success, I was deeply depressed and unhappy.

I began gaining weight. My personal relationships were in turmoil. Communications with my business partner were terrible. Literally, I was out of control.

Me, early 1990s

I knew something needed to change. But, I was floundering, unable to figure out which direction to go, lost in a maze of frustration, anger, and disappointment. I was really having difficulty coming to terms with the fact that I was no longer going to be a star athlete. Instead, I was stuck in a supportive role to other athletes having great careers. It sucked!

Finally, I realized that I couldn't keep living with the intense internal and life struggle I'd been going through for a couple of years. I had to admit to myself that I needed help. Me, the guy who had all the answers for other people who needed help, but not for myself. I tried to ignore the frustration and pain in my life, but I just couldn't take it any longer. I was a mental and emotional wreck, and was reaching the end of my rope.

Not being able to see any other options, I made the life-changing decision that I couldn't live this way anymore. As luck would have it, I heard about a one-day training course on communication. I went to it praying something would shift — and it did.

At the end of that day, I felt like I'd been thrown a life line — and I caught it. For the first time in my life, I realized I could control my emotions and thoughts in ways I never thought possible. I now had some tools to get better at communicating and operating in life. I had hope!

After the course, I spoke to the lead trainer, Gary, and explained my situation and struggles to him. My apprehension was palpable and he could clearly see that I was deeply struggling. I think he intuitively knew that it was very difficult for me just to ask for help. After our discussion, he suggested some coaching and, on the spot, I hired him as my first coach.

In our first session, I discovered the one thing that I had been blind to my entire life. Gary masterfully showed me that I had been living with the subconscious belief that I was not good enough. I was amazed as he helped me see that it was all because of programming — shame and powerlessness — from when I was a child: living on food stamps, housing support, being skinny, being called giraffe, feeling less than because of my economic status, having divorced parents, growing up fatherless, being labeled a troublemaker and loser. Though sports were my passion and developed me in many positive ways, they had also become my cover up, my way of masking and hiding from those beliefs. For the first time in my life, I realized and could see that all that programing wasn't true.

Gary helped me see the "blind spot" I'd been living with my entire life. With this new understanding and the tools Gary provided me, things immediately began to shift in my life. As I continued the coaching sessions, my life improved.

During one session with Gary, I was reminded of my boxing coach, Tom Delaney. I had walked into my first boxing gym when I turned 18 (my Mom wouldn't let me box until I was 18). I remember hearing the speed bags rattle, the ring buzzer going off, the smell of sweat, and the scent of Old Spice cologne (an interesting combination).

I was immediately drawn to Tom Delaney, an Irish gentleman about age 50. He was 5'10" with pinkish skin and he had a bit of a beer belly. He began coaching me. He could see something in me that I couldn't see in myself and over time, he helped shape me into a confident and competitive boxer. He had a unique way of being completely present in the moment, compassionate and making me feel safe, even though he was coaching in the very violent and competitive world of boxing.

I didn't realize it at the time, but Tom was to become my model of a great coach: He had a sense about him of always being present and knew exactly what to say no matter what the situation. He knew how to connect specifically to me. There was always a sense of feeling safe in his presence and at the same time, he knew how to gently push me to be better. I always felt he had my back and was in my corner no matter if I won or lost. That didn't matter. He was truly a coach that had only one intention and that was for me to be the best I could be in the ring and out.

I learned many life lessons in those years of Tom's guidance and I still do when I return to Chicago and have those special moments talking over coffee with my coach and friend.

Me and Tom Delaney, Christmas 2014

"I believe everyone needs a Tom Delaney, someone who is in your corner no matter what and sees you for who you truly are."
— Steven Griffith

With coaching from Gary and new reflections of the impact Tom was having on me as a coach, I now began to embrace my true purpose in life: the role of being a coach, advisor, and support for others so they could reach their full potential. In the process, I was doing the same for myself.

I remember Gary saying, "If you follow the coaching, your life will change. If you continue to do what you've been doing, you will have the same results you've been having. It's your choice." In all honesty, I was unsure if I could change and was afraid that it might not work.

Well, I followed the coaching and it did work. I lost the weight I'd gained and my personal relationships began to improve. Interactions with my clients got better and my business grew. It was the first time I was really happy and legitimately hopeful about my life and future. It had been a long time since I'd last felt hopeful. The chains of my past were broken, chains I'd not even known I'd had. I was no longer blind to my Blind Spot (it's hard to change it if you can't see it).

Gary's coaching had such a profound impact on me. I started studying everything I could on peak performance, psychology and communication, as well as training with the top people in those fields, so I could help others like Gary had helped me.

I also realized I had this laboratory filled with world-class athletes, elite business executives, and celebrities. Pulling from what I had learned from the top professionals in peak performance, communication and the science behind performance, I refined, shortened, streamlined, and simplified those tools and techniques over the next ten years to create the highest performance in the shortest amount of time. I took the very best of everything, kept what worked, threw out what didn't, and the end result: The High Performance Coaching System — simple to use, science-based, maximum results.

> "Whether in the boardroom or on the playing field, the difference between a home run and a strike lies more in one's mind than in one's swing."
> — Steven Griffith

With the success I was having, people started coming to me from outside of the health and fitness world for coaching. I realized it was time for me to help a larger group of people. Fifteen years ago, I sold my interest in the gym and started High Performance Coaching.

So, what I learned from my journey to High Performance Coaching was that I had a Blind Spot that I didn't even know I had. We all have them: Blind Spots that actually stop us from seeing opportunities and that create roadblocks to our true selves. Once I knew my Blind Spot, I could actually resolve it, change, and start living the life I was meant to lead, not the life my past had programmed for me. I now had the ability to help others do the same thing in a very short period of time with my HPC System. They would no longer have to endure the pain and suffering of living a life in their Blind Spot instead of the life they were destined to lead.

How about you? What's your Blind Spot? What's holding you back from your own personal and business High Performance?

It's time to let go of what's holding you back so can have the career, money, freedom, relationships, and health and wellness you deserve — a life that's true to your life purpose.

So, if you are ready, join thousands of people just like you to see what you haven't seen before. Let me help you identify your Blind Spot and together help you have a breakthrough!

# Chapter 2

# THE FOUNDATION OF HIGH PERFORMANCE COACHING

*"Learn the fundamentals of the game and stick to them. Band-aid remedies never last."*

— Jack Nicklaus,
Legendary Professional Golfer

High Performance Coaching (HPC) is not therapy or life coaching. It is a performance system that bridges the gap from your potential and what's holding you back to your own personal High Performance.

What most people don't realize is that they are missing out on their true potential because of Blind Spots that they don't even know they have, negative conditioning from the past (we'll go more deeply into this in Chapter 4). For now, all you need to know is that these Blind Spots create a misalignment with your beliefs, values, communication, and your life purpose that create underperformance. The HPC System identifies your Blind Spot and aligns your beliefs, values, communication, and life purpose for a breakthrough.

The HPC System is illustrated by the pyramid on the next page, which I created many years ago. Step 1 begins with your BELIEFS. These are the core ideas and concepts that create whatever possibilities or limitations you have. It all comes down to what you believe internally. Some of your beliefs are at the conscious level and some at the subconscious level (based mainly on your early childhood programming and life events.) So, first we identify the limiting beliefs that are holding you back from truly having what you want in your life.

Once your limiting beliefs are identified, we break through your Blind Spot and old ways of thinking, create new beliefs that support you, and allow you to move into the next process that I guide you through, which is identifying your life purpose: what's truly important to you personally and professionally and why. Once that's been identified, you then move on to Step 2 in the HPC System.

The High Performance Pyramid

In Step 2, we drop down to the right corner of the pyramid to VALUES.

VALUES are the things that are important to you, your ultimate goals in life. What's really and truly important to you? Where do you spend your time, money, and energy? Establishing the correct hierarchy of your values becomes part of your HPC System blueprint.

Every decision you make, every place you invest your time, money, and energy is then reflected by your values.

Once your values are aligned, we then move across the bottom of the pyramid to the left corner to Step 3, COMMUNICATION, where you effectively align and focus in a positive way on your internal self-talk, regulate your emotions, and learn to speak successfully in the world. What's your self-talk? What is the old story that has been directing your thoughts and emotions?

This is where we implement mindfulness (which we'll go into in greater detail in the next chapter): present, moment-to-moment awareness without judgment. Utilizing this concept, I will teach you new skills for managing your thoughts and emotions and thinking and responding rationally rather than reacting emotionally so you can create the results you want.

Once we have your beliefs, values, communication and life purpose aligned, great things begin to happen. You will have the opportunity to experience more dynamic health, positive relationships, increased financial success, mindful living, greater happiness, and what most of us ultimately desire, that sense of freedom to do what we want, when we want to be free from the obstacles of the past.

# Chapter 3

# THE SCIENCE BEHIND HIGH PERFORMANCE COACHING

*"Things do not change; we change."*
— Henry David Thoreau,
American Author, Poet, and Philosopher

In this chapter, I have simplified the complex findings from all my research into an easy-to-use, science-based system — The New Science of Performance — that creates real-world results.

## Mindfulness

One of the foundational principles at the core of HPC is mindfulness. With each concept, you will learn how being mindful allows everything to be accelerated. Mindfulness in its simplest form means to pay complete attention to the present moment without judgment.

Being more mindful comes down to being present with your own inner experience with full sensory awareness. This full awareness is about taking a step back from your thoughts, feelings, and sensations to gain a bigger perspective on your sense of self.

In this practice, you learn to just watch the contents of your mind in a present, calm, and non-reactive way — like sitting in a movie theater comfortably watching the big screen knowing that it's just a movie and you don't have to respond to what's happening on the screen.

You learn to just be with your thoughts and feelings as they arise. You will learn to accept thoughts as just thoughts and feelings as just feelings. They will come and go and that's okay. As you practice mindfulness over time, you will find it becomes possible (and even easy) to accept whatever thoughts arise, positive or negative, without taking action or reacting to them emotionally. When this happens, a process of responding rationally versus reacting emotionally begins to occur. You get the the results you want whether it's in business — selling, negotiating, managing, or relationship building — or in your personal life when it comes to parenting, intimate relationships, and making the right decisions for you and your family's health and wellness.

In the big picture, when you begin to implement mindfulness in all aspects of your life, you are no longer controlled by automatic negative thoughts or emotions that don't serve you. This allows you to create a new High Performance future, one that is not controlled by your past.

Through the HPC System, you will develop mindfulness skills, learning to respond rather than react to old belief and behavior patterns. Scientific research supports dozens of positive effects from implementing mindfulness, i.e.,

- seeing your true self
- diminishing and managing stress
- decreasing anxiety, pain, and depression
- increasing cognitive functioning
- increased happiness
- increased performance
- positive brain chemistry changes
- having greater emotional regulation
- greater engagement
- increased empathy and compassion

> "Mindfulness practice means that we commit fully in each moment to be present; inviting ourselves to interface with this moment in full awareness...."
>
> — Jon Kabat-Zinn,
> Mindfulness Leader
> and Developer of the Mind-Body
> Stress Reduction Program (MBSR)

The byproduct of this process is more energy, aliveness and connection to your true self and purpose, and greater business and personal performance.

## The Ability to Change

Your biology is not your destiny. In *The Brain That Changes Itself*, Dr. Norman Doidge reports through dozens of research studies and real-life stories that the brain is a plastic, living organ that can actually change its own structure and function, even in old age.

Arguably, the most important breakthrough in neuroscience since scientists first sketched out the brain's basic anatomy, this revolutionary discovery — called neuroplasticity — promises to overthrow the centuries-old notion that the brain is fixed and unchanging. The brain is not, as was thought, like a machine or "hardwired" like a computer. Dr. Doidge has shown that what and how we think can change our brains. He has illuminated the foundations of psychological healing:

"What makes neuroplasticity so exciting is that this completely upends how we look at the brain. This means that the brain, far from being a collection of specialized parts, each fixed in its location and function, is in fact a dynamic organ — an organ that can re-wire and rearrange itself as the need arises. This is an insight from which all of us can benefit.

> "We have learned that our thoughts can switch our genes on and off, altering our brain anatomy."
> — Norman Doidge, Author,
> *The Brain that Changed Itself*

"People with severe afflictions, i.e., strokes, cerebral palsy, schizophrenia, learning disabilities, obsessive compulsive disorders and the like, are the most obvious candidates, but who among us would not like to tack on a few IQ points or improve our memories?"

Doidge outlines the brain's ability to reorganize itself by forming new neural connections throughout life. Through numerous case studies, he describes stroke victims who have learned to move and speak again, senior citizens who have sharpened their memories, and children who have raised their IQs and overcome learning disabilities, among others. This science, he predicts, will have ramifications for professionals in many fields, but especially for teachers of all types.

I am sure you are familiar with the old belief that our genetics are to blame: our IQ is set in stone, so to speak. You are stuck and there is only so far you can go.

I have seen people with self-defeating and limiting beliefs such as "Oh, this is just how I am," or "I don't have the talent," and so on. But when a person applies sustained effort over time, research shows he or she can outperform people with higher IQs and more talent by just staying the course.

High Performance Coaching helps you create that sustained effort by aligning your beliefs, values, and communication.

Once your values and beliefs are aligned, you learn how to apply the correct communication that supports them. You will discover how to handle stress and learn to regulate your emotions and persist in performing at your highest level regardless of your genetics and circumstances.

# Perseverance, Passion,
## and Courage in the Face of Adversity

This reminds me of a story I heard a while back. Harrison Ford had gone to Hollywood with a group of other actors to embark on his career. Later, during an interview, he was asked, "How is it that you became successful?" Ford responded, "I was the last man standing."

Angela Duckworth's research on grit at the University of Pennsylvania has uncovered something interesting on this topic: perseverance, passion, and courage in the face of adversity. When she studied top composers, doctors, spelling bee champions, West Point cadets and other high-level performers, she discovered that while talent and IQ are factors, what's more important is that the sustained application of effort over time is one of the single greatest determining factors of success.

There is something to be said for persistence and grit, yet what stands in the way for so many people? At the end of day, it's distraction. People are unable to maintain their focus on what's really important to them: their values.

In today's world, we're faced with a tremendous amount of distraction from TV, media messaging, and the use of technology. Technology, with all its conveniences, can also be a great barrier.

When you can overcome distractions and focus on your goals day in and day out, moment by moment so that each thought, action, behavior and decision moves you toward them, great things will happen for you. Persistence and focus always overcome challenges and failures.

High Performance Coaching is based on one basic principle: simple instructions to keep you focused for fast, real-world results. The more you integrate with the HPC System, the more your brain re-programs itself, changes mental and emotional patterns, and creates the results you want in your life.

Your ultimate success comes down to stopping, starting, or changing behavior. From their book *Influencer*, Kerry Patterson, Joseph Grenny, David Maxfield, Ron McMillan, and Al Switzler found from over ten years of research that two things have to happen for change:

1. You have to believe that what you want is worth the effort.

2. You have to believe you can do it (on your own or with an advocate, educator, or coach).

You must be ready to answer "yes" to these two statements above.

When you can clearly see what you want and need to do, your perseverance becomes even more activated.

# Small Steps to Change,
# The Kaizen Method

> ## "Whoever wants to reach a distant goal must take small steps."
> — Saul Bellow,
> Pulitzer Prize-winning Author

The Japanese "Kaizen Method" means taking "small steps." Small steps can make fast changes. The Kaizen theory was written about by one of the top experts in the field, Robert Maurer, PhD. He wrote the book, *One Small Step Can Change Your Life, The Kaizen Way*. Small steps are what we take in High Performance Coaching, creating small steps in a way that bypasses the fear center in the brain — the limbic center — where the amygdale (ah-mig'dah-lah) exists. The amygdale is our fight, flight, or freeze center.

When we create small steps, whether it's focusing on a specific goal, increasing our performance in our jobs or improving the quality of our relationships and focusing on our habits, we bypass the fear center. Our new behaviors create new neuro-pathways in our brains that allow us to get fast results.

Think about a man who wants to lose a hundred pounds. When he looks at the challenge in his mind's eye, he sees, "I've got to lose 100 pounds," and he's paralyzed. Fear takes over and he freezes. If we first asked this same man to walk to the front door and back, he could do that.

The next day, we'd ask him to walk down to his car and back and before you know it, the guy is walking seven miles a day and 100 pounds are gone. I've seen clients lose 100 pounds with nothing more than the idea of small steps. It's about creating new habits — talking small steps.

The High Performance System is about focusing on habits. When we put new, positive habits together, we have a whole new nervous system that creates massive results.

## Positive Psychology

Another researcher whose work is in alignment and incorporated with High Performance Coaching is Martin Seligman at the University of Pennsylvania, one of the fathers of positive psychology. He talks about how to flourish and wrote the books *Flourish* and *Authentic Happiness.*

Seligman has come up with an acronym — PERMA — for the principles of how to flourish beyond just happiness:

- "P" stands for creating Positive emotions
- "E" stands for being Engaged or Engagement
- "R" is Relationships
- "M" is having Meaning
- "A" is Accomplishments

When all of these are present and in balance, we flourish. Seligman's research also supports that when you have an optimistic view, you flourish. High Performance Coaching is an advocate of an optimistic view and promotes the PERMA way of being.

When you remove your Blind Spots and align your values and purpose, you have engagement, fulfilling relationships and purpose in your life, which produces accomplishments.

## Cultivating Positivity

In conjunction with Seligman's work, Barbara Fredrickson, who wrote the book *Positivity*, is a PhD psychologist at the University of North Carolina at Chapel Hill. She is also the director of the Positive Emotions and Physiological Laboratory, a.k.a. the PEP Lab. What she found is something very interesting.

Fredrickson studies the relationship of positive emotions versus negative emotions. She performed years of research and discovered that when a person has a three to one ratio of positive emotions to negative emotions, they flourish.

She says, "We all know that negativity is in every part of the news, TV shows, and negativity pervades your self-talk, and it leaks into relationships at home, at work, even to people you don't even know, but what happens when that's pervasive, there's a shutting down of our natural kindness and compassion for ourselves and others." That can be with our clients, colleagues, friends, and family.

On top of that negativity, it also creates health damaging negative emotions, like anger, resentment and depression, which can affect the entire body causing the release of cortisol. Cortisol production can create muscle tension, blood pressure increase, increased respiration, heart rate increase, and the inability to recover from normal stress.

When you change negative emotions to positive ones, you really begin to flourish. When you do that, your state of mind can really enhance your relationships, improve your health, improve your performance, and broaden your mind. We'll discuss this some more in Chapter 9.

So, Barbara Fredrickson's seminal research really sets the stage for the work that I do with people in getting their internal state very positive, creating momentum, and moving toward their goals and purpose in life.

From Barbara's and many others' research involving thousands of subjects, the following emotions were most prevalent.

- Joy
- Gratitude
- Serenity
- Interest
- Hope

- Pride
- Amusement
- Inspiration
- Awe
- Love

> "If the goal is to have more happiness, we need to focus in on how to create more triggers that create positive emotions."
> — Steven Griffith

What is most important when looking at these particular emotions is to focus on the triggers that turn on the emotion, rather than just the feelings of them. For example: "When I see my daughter play basketball, I have a deep sense of gratitude." The trigger is watching her play basketball.

When we are focused on positivity and purpose, less of our energy is wasted. Suddenly, our true self emerges, our performance improves, and our propensity for kindness and compassion spills into the world.

# An Old Cherokee Tale of Two Wolves

One evening, an old Cherokee Indian told his grandson about a battle that goes on inside people. He said, "My son, the battle is between two 'wolves' inside us all. One is Evil. It is anger, envy, jealousy, sorrow, regret, greed, arrogance, self-pity, guilt, resentment, inferiority, lies, false pride, superiority, and ego. The other is good. It is joy, peace, love, hope, serenity, humility, kindness, benevolence, empathy, generosity, truth, compassion, and faith."

The grandson thought about it for a minute and then asked his grandfather, "Which wolf wins?"

The old Cherokee simply replied, "The one you feed."

This is such a lovely story: so simple and yet so true. I think each and every one of us has these two wolves running around inside us. The Evil Wolf or the Good Wolf is fed daily by the choices we make with our thoughts. Just as you learned with Barbara Fredrickson's work, what you think about and dwell upon will, in a sense, appear in your life and influence your behavior.

We have a choice: Feed the Good Wolf and it will show up in our character, habits, and behavior positively; or feed the Evil Wolf and our whole world will turn negative. The crucial question is, "Which wolf are you feeding today?"

# Chapter 4

# STEP 1 — BELIEFS & BLIND SPOTS

*"Whether you believe you can or you believe you can't, either way you're right."*

— Henry Ford, American Industrialist

S tep 1 of the 3-Step HPC System is about aligning your beliefs to what you truly want in life. You now know that the first step is identifying what limiting beliefs are holding you back. Many of our beliefs were created early in childhood and, through life events, continually affect our ongoing successes and failures.

The High Performance Pyramid

We also have beliefs being founded via the media. An example is the recent financial crisis. Many people believe they can or cannot do something because of the economy or some other looming national predicament. The media makes money by gaining viewers and bad news sells so they bombard people with "It's doomsday." Look back at the days of Napoleon Hill and *Think and Grow Rich*. There were more millionaires created in the Great Depression of the 20th century than any time before in history.

There is never a better time in history right now to break through and get what you want in this age of technology and instant information.

> "You can be anything you want to be, if only you believe with sufficient conviction and act in accordance with your faith; for whatever the mind can conceive and believe, the mind can achieve."
>
> — Napoleon Hill, Author,
> *Think and Grow Rich*

Beliefs are ideas or core concepts about ourselves. Each time we take action, make a decision or even think, our minds refer to a Rolodex™ of our life events. Then our thoughts follow a familiar pattern and create positive or negative results.

Every choice we are faced with is checked consciously and subconsciously in our mental Rolodex. If the records of past events tell us we cannot do something, we believe it!

# It's Not Your Fault

There is a vicious cycle between our beliefs, our actions, and our results. Our beliefs direct our actions and we take actions to support our beliefs. When our beliefs are misaligned, our potential and performance are often severely limited and we don't achieve the results we desire. If you're not performing at your highest level, it's not your fault — and here's why.

What most people don't realize is that they are missing out on their true potential because of Blind Spots that they don't even know they have.

Your Blind Spots are created from negative conditioning from your past. Blind Spots are diversions created by your subconscious mind, designed to keep you "safe," comfortable, and not taking risks. We all have them...if there is a gap from where you want to be and actually are, there is a Blind Spot stopping you from performing at your highest level.

As I said earlier, I've learned in my years of coaching people just like you — entrepreneurs, business owners, CEOs, executives, celebrities, athletes, and entertainment professionals — is that there are "hidden roadblocks" keeping you stuck and struggling and they are Blind Spots. It's what I call the Performance Gap.

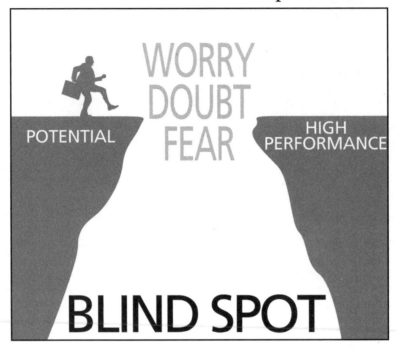

**There is something you are not seeing. And you cannot change what you cannot see.**

Because of this, your subconscious mind is programming you to take the safe and familiar road because you are conditioned to not see opportunities and options. Instead, you block out the opportunities and remain stuck, frustrated, under-performing, and not accelerating at the pace and speed you know you can in business and life. The Blind Spot is created from your limiting beliefs and becomes intertwined with them.

You must ask yourself, "Who do I need to be to have what I want?" and "What belief is stopping me from having it?" That is the doorway to breaking through the limiting beliefs and Blind Spot that are keeping you stuck. For example, if you have been financially stuck, not advancing in your career at the pace you know you can, have continued weight and wellness issues or continue to struggle in relationships, these are all based on who you are being or not being, which is all connected to the limiting beliefs you hold and your Blind Spot.

So, if you are not activating the strategies and motivations to get what you want and are not being who you need to be to have it, it doesn't matter what goal, purpose, or vision you have in your life. To take this one step further, if you just focus on changing your actions and behaviors and not the limiting beliefs behind them, you'll get a temporary fix at best, but in actuality be stuck forever and never break out of your Blind Spot.

The truth is that if you want to grow to your full potential and excel, you have to identify your Blind Spot and break free of it!

## Here's How Blind Spots are Created

As I said before, Blind Spots are conditioned patterns from when we were young and our life events that created the neural wiring of whether we believe we can or can't do something. Our past programming literally wires our set point for success — how successful we will be in our career, the money we make, the quality of our relationships, our health and wellness, etc.

The good news is that you can change your set point and I'm going to show you exactly how to do that later in this chapter.

Let's take a look at how a Blind Spot is created. The following is a model adapted from Dr. Thurman Fleet who in the 1930s developed one of the first explanations and diagrams that I like to use to clearly explain how the conscious and subconscious mind work and how a Blind Spot is created.

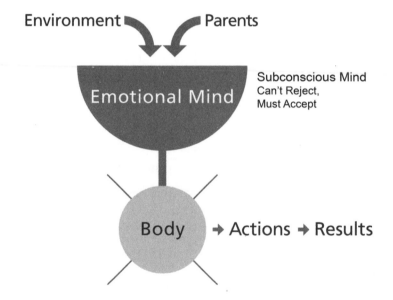

The subconscious mind, what's considered the emotional mind, is wide open from ages 0 – 7. As you can see from the diagram, the mind is like an open container. It has no ability to reject information — it must accept everything. The messages you received from your parents and caregivers — what you could or couldn't do, what is safe or not safe, what is right or wrong, if you're smart or not smart, if you're good enough or not good enough, whether you're lovable or not, whether you're attractive or not, who you're supposed to be or not be — programmed your subconscious mind with limiting beliefs without you even knowing.

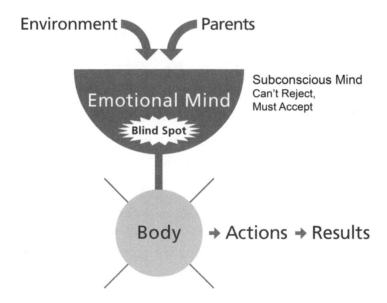

Whatever your environment consisted of: trauma and drama, stress, fear, and/or anxiety — that all has an impact on your beliefs. As you can see illustrated in the diagram on the previous page, your Blind Spot is embedded in your subconscious mind and shielding you from knowing what's holding you back (your limiting beliefs that were created that you don't even know you have). *And if you can't see it, you can't change it.*

This is not about blaming your parents or the people who raised you. This is just understanding that your environment shaped you. Your parents and caregivers did the best they could with what they had no matter what the circumstances you were raised in.

As you read this, your Blind Spot is going to try and stop you from understanding it, so I'm going to say this again: Blind Spots are created from beliefs that are not true, but that you *believe* to be true. The very nature of Blind Spots means you can't see them. It is very difficult if not nearly impossible to see them on your own — *and you cannot change what you cannot see.*

Let's continue looking at how your operating system (your mind) was developed and works.

The conscious mind (thinking mind) is the opposite in its function of the subconscious mind, which allows us to accept, reject, and reason. It allows us to have free choice and decide how and where to spend our time, energy, and money.

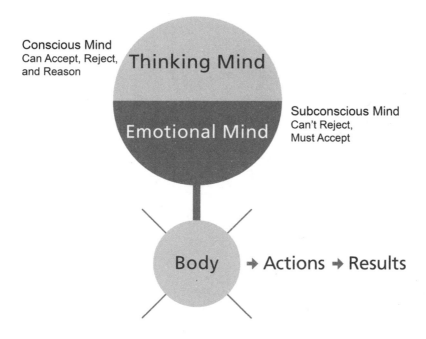

So, here is the truth of the situation: As you go through life day to day making career decisions and choices about relationships, your health and wellness, finances, etc. — all those choices appear as free choice, a conscious choice, but in reality, *your subconscious mind is telling your conscious mind how to think, act, and feel.*

In actuality, the subconscious mind is running the show. So, you go through life thinking you are making conscious choices while all along those choices are subconsciously driven by your past. That is why you can so clearly see what other people's problems and challenges are and how to fix them, but are blind to your own. Now you know.

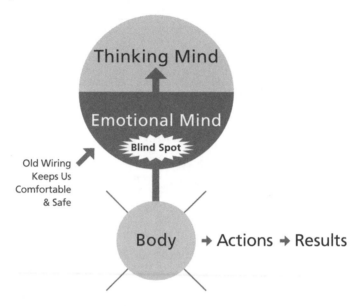

Your Blind Spot is working 24/7 to keep you subconsciously safe and comfortable and avoiding pain regardless of what's happening in your conscious world. It will cause you to be illogical, irrational, stop you from seeing opportunities, and will ultimately hold you back. Many people are consciously unhappy, don't know why they're stuck, and are not moving forward at the pace and speed they know they can. They keep doing what they shouldn't be doing. It's almost as if there were an invisible force holding them back. It's not invisible, it's their Blind Spot.

Not to worry. My High Performance Coaching System will help you identify the limiting beliefs behind your Blind Spot, establish your true purpose, values and goals, then shift and align your beliefs so that your thoughts, emotions, and actions support your goals. You will now have the tools to choose a different path, one that takes you from your high potential to your High Performance in business and in life.

**Breakthrough to High Performance**

↑

**Create and Activate New Strategies**

↑

**Bring to Consciousness**

↑

**Identify Blind Spot
(Limiting Beliefs)**

> "If you limit your choices only to what seems possible or reasonable, you disconnect yourself from what you truly want, and all that is left is a compromise."
>
> — Robert Fritz, Author,
> *Path of Least Resistance*

Our beliefs dictate how we relate to others, how we view the world, and how we perform.

Over the next few chapters, we are going to look at the core steps to identifying, programming, and activating new powerful beliefs that shift with very simple instructions and that break you through to the next level.

Here are a few stories from my coaching about how identifying and changing your limiting beliefs can free you from your Blind Spot and change your life forever.

One of the stories that come to mind is a recent client, Cindy. Cindy was a high-level executive in the entertainment industry. She came to me because she was struggling in a career in which she had invested many years. Because of her investment, she felt she had to keep going, although her passion was gone. She came to me in complete dismay because she had just sold her huge dream house in Malibu, California, and wasn't doing well personally. As I started talking to her, my question was, "Wow, what is all this drama around the house?" We began working at the top of the pyramid about her beliefs just as I do with all my clients.

*"What's going on with this house?"* I asked. *"What does the house represent to you?"*

"Well, being successful," Cindy responded.

*"What belief do you have about yourself for that to be true?"* I asked.

As she spoke, she revealed her belief. "I don't feel I'm good enough unless I have this really huge impressive house."

We identified her belief that the house symbolized success and how that had been deceiving her to stay in a job where she felt there was no way out. This limiting belief had been with her throughout her entire life.

Cindy grew up without much and a house was always a symbol of success in her neighborhood. That had been wired into her belief system. Once we identified that, she eventually bought a new home in Malibu that was one-half the value of the previous Malibu home and she was much happier. She saw where she had been making decisions her whole life based on the value of external material things such as the house and other items that weren't really that important. This previous lifestyle caused a tremendous amount of stress as she was constantly overextending herself financially.

"Wow, those beliefs had been a ball and chain preventing freedom in my life," she proclaimed.

Another client, John, had been a successful CEO of a technology company. When he came to me, his dissatisfaction was with his current relationship.

"I have been with her for five years. We are both fifty, but she is getting old." As he continued, his comments were all about her, she this and she that. I asked him to bring a picture of her on his next visit.

A few weeks later, John brought a picture of his girlfriend to me. She was beautiful, very youthful looking, and fit. I looked at this picture and listened to what he was telling me and realized something was not in alignment with his beliefs. So, we began examining his beliefs.

*"Let's not focus on her, let's focus on you. What belief do you have about a girlfriend?"*

"Well, I believe that I should have a really beautiful, vibrant girlfriend, or future wife," John answered.

*"Hmmm…the picture seems to show that you have a beautiful girlfriend. What are you holding true about yourself that you feel you need somebody younger?"*

As we talked, I helped John uncover his belief, "I don't feel good enough unless I have somebody who's young next to me."

Going more deeply into our discussion and working together, we eventually identified John's belief that he felt inadequate unless he had a really beautiful, young, sexy girl next to him. He believed this was a symbol of his level of status. He was retired and had a lot of money and felt he should have a trophy wife, but was in conflict about it. He was with someone who deeply loved and cared about him who was also very beautiful.

His limiting beliefs of not being good enough were interfering with his feelings for his girlfriend. As we worked together and shifted his beliefs, and, later, his values, he started creating new belief patterns about his self-esteem and self-worth. By doing so, he began to focus on what was truly important to him in a relationship. He developed a deeply connected relationship with his present girlfriend, became engaged, and is now happily married. He had been in a Blind Spot and now he could see what he couldn't see before.

As I mentioned earlier, as I was growing up, I focused all of my attention on getting bigger and stronger. Although athletic, I was a tall and skinny kid and didn't fully come into my body until age 19 or 20. My belief system told me that my success in the world and self-esteem were based on sports and how big and tough and strong I could be. Later, when my football and boxing career ended, I found myself in no man's land and didn't know what to do or who I was.

Although I went on to have a great career owning my own business working with top Olympic and professional athletes, my own personal Blind Spot was holding me back. While on the outside

I looked like I had everything, on the inside I felt empty and worthless. I felt like no one would really love me or respect me because I was no longer an athlete.

That's when I met my first coach and uncovered my Blind Spot, which brought into alignment my beliefs, values, and purpose. That motivated and propelled me over the next ten years to creating the High Performance Coaching System. Essentially, I identified my false and limiting beliefs. I had been living my life pretending, and when that shifted, everything shifted.

## Breaking Through Your Limiting Beliefs

I have worked with thousands of people taking them through my Blind Spot Breakthrough System™ (BSBS™) so they can have a High Performance life. My clients have experienced breakthroughs over and over using this process.

The fastest way to break through the limiting beliefs that are holding you back in your career, finances, relationships, and health and wellness is using the BSBS process, which begins by asking the question, "Who do I need to be to have what I want?" Ask this question about any area of your personal or business performance where you're stuck, have slowed down, or stalled out and want to break through to the next level.

As you have previously learned, your limiting beliefs are many times held subconsciously out of your awareness because of your Blind

Spot. They are the major cause of your underperformance. The BSBS process rapidly uncovers the limiting beliefs that are holding you back and allows you to accelerate your personal breakthrough.

Here are the questions for you to ask in the process:

1. "Who do I need to be to have what I want?"

2. "What belief am I holding about myself that keeps me from being _____ (answer from #1)."

3. "What belief am I holding about myself that makes this true?" (Answer from #2.)

4. "Is this belief really true? Am I 100% sure this belief is true? Is it true 100% of the time?"

Here's an example of the BSBS process in action with one of my clients who was stuck in his career and finances:

Step 1 – Question: Who do I need to be to have what I want? (Example: Who do I need to be to have what I want *in order to advance in my career and make more money?*)

Answer: "I need to be more confident and assertive in business."

Step 2 – Question: What belief am I holding about myself that keeps me from being confident and assertive?

Answer: "I don't have the right education."

Step 3 – Question: What belief am I holding about myself that makes this true?

Answer: "I'm not smart enough."

Question: What belief am I holding about myself that makes this true?

Answer: "I'm not good enough."

My client came to the realization that the limiting belief holding him back was "I'm not good enough."

Now that he had identified his limiting belief, to finish the process and to get to his breakthrough, I then instructed him to ask himself:

Step 4 – Is it really true that I'm not good enough? (Yes or no.) He answered "no." If he had answered "yes," then I would have instructed him to ask himself, "Am I 100% sure this belief is true?" "Is it true 100% of the time?"

You may have to repeatedly go through the process of asking these questions — you may even repeat your answers — until you intuitively get to the limiting belief of what's holding you back. Remember, your Blind Spot is creating resistance to keep you from uncovering the truth. This is totally normal. This process may take a little time, so, if you're feeling stuck, just be patient and stay with it, you will get there.

Now it's time to identify your limiting belief using the BSBS process. Answer each of the questions as they relate to your specific goal or area where you desire a breakthrough in your career, finances, relationships, or health and wellness.

1. Who do I need to be to have what I want?

_____

_____

_____

_____

_____

_____

_____

_____

_____

_____

_____

_____

2. What belief am I holding about myself that keeps me from being (Use your answer from #1.)?

_____

_____

_____

_____

_____

_____

_____

_____

_____

_____

_____

3. What belief am I holding about myself that makes this true? (Use your answer from #2. Repeat the question as necessary.)

_____

_____

_____

_____

_____

_____

_____

_____

_____

_____

_____

_____

_____

_____

4. Is this belief really true? Am I 100% sure this belief is true? Is it true 100% of the time?

_____

_____

_____

_____

_____

_____

_____

_____

_____

_____

_____

_____

Now that you have identified your limiting belief that has been holding you back, you are ready to reprogram your mind and create new strategies to your ultimate High Performance. As you move forward, your Blind Spot may become activated causing worry, doubt, and fear. By being aware of your limiting belief, turning it around and creating a new and powerful positive belief, you will automatically be operating from prosperity, abundance, and love. When these conditions are present, you naturally perform at your highest level.

## Turning Your Limiting Belief Around

It's time to turn your limiting belief around to support you in your new strategies and actions propelling you to success. To do this, I like to use a process I learned from Jack Canfield to turn limiting beliefs around into positive statements that support your new, positive beliefs.

Canfield says we must give ourselves "the permission to have it." That's really a big deal, having permission. He says, "...all your inner dialogue and outer conversations should be aimed at getting to where you want to be, so keep replacing any thought or belief that is keeping you from achieving your goals with an empowering thought or belief that will take you closer to your goals."

> "You can overcome any limiting belief. You make the shift in thinking that can mean the difference between a lifetime of 'could haves' versus accomplishments."
>
> — Jack Canfield, Co-author, *Chicken Soup for the Soul* book series

Here are Canfield's steps to Overcoming Any Limiting Belief,[1] to which I've added an additional step.

Use the following questions and your answers to turn any limiting beliefs into empowering ones.

(Using the limiting belief you previously identified in the BSBS process, proceed with Step One of his process.)

---

[1] Canfield, Jack, *The Success Principles: How to Get from Where You Are to Where You Want to Be,* Harper, 2005.

**Step One:** Write down the limiting belief you identified in the BSBS process that is holding you back from getting what you want. (I've provided space here for you to break through multiple beliefs that may be holding you back. Proceed through the five steps one limiting belief at a time.)

Example: I am not smart enough.

_____

_____

_____

_____

_____

_____

_____

_____

_____

_____

**Step Two:** Write a statement about how that belief is limiting you.

Example: Because I am not smart enough, I cannot attract a good mate, advance in my career, or budget by money.

_____

_____

_____

_____

_____

_____

_____

_____

_____

_____

_____

_____

**Step Three:** Write a statement about the way you want to be, think, feel, and act after you shift your limiting belief.

Example: I am smart enough and have the confidence that I will attract the right mate, get a promotion, and take control of my money and life.

_____

_____

_____

_____

_____

_____

_____

_____

_____

_____

**Step Four:** Create a turnaround statement that gives you permission to be, act, feel, and think to do this.

Example: I am intelligent and in charge of my life, and make the right decisions to be successful. What other people have said or think of me does not matter.

_____

_____

_____

_____

_____

_____

_____

_____

_____

_____

**Step Five:** Describe what your life looks like and how you feel after your limiting belief is shifted.

Example: My life is moving smoothly, I feel at peace, I achieve my goals, and I am deeply fulfilled.

_____

_____

_____

_____

_____

_____

_____

_____

_____

_____

_____

_____

# Chapter 5

# YOUR LIFE PURPOSE

*"The two most important days of your
life are the day you were born and
the day you find out why."*
— Mark Twain

*"I believe for each of us to be successful, we need
to take the time to strip away the layers
to determine who we truly are and who we
need to be in order to honor our life purpose.
This is the ultimate first step to performing
at your highest level in business and in life.
Without this, you will aimlessly move from one
path, one career, and one relationship
to another and never engage in your
authentic purpose and full potential."*
— Steven Griffith

# Why You Should Find Your Life Purpose

**1. Your life purpose gives meaning to everything you do.**

Your life purpose makes everything you do *meaningful*. You could be successful on the outside, but if you are not internally aligned with your purpose, you will never truly feel satisfied in life.

**2. Your life purpose directs and guides you.**

Not only can your life purpose give you meaning, it can also give you clear direction as to where to go in life. This helps you make big decisions. People who never find their life purpose lack a strong foundation upon which to make their decisions. They most likely will follow popular opinions influenced by the Internet, television, other media, and friends and family.

Besides helping you make big decisions, your life purpose can also guide you in making small decisions. When you have two options in front of you, choosing what is best for you is easier when you know what your life purpose is.

**3. Your life purpose motivates you.**

In life, there will be difficult times to go through. You may experience failure or rejection. In such situations, your life purpose can give you the motivation you need to keep going.

How can your life purpose do that? By helping you see beyond the horizon. What you face in front of you may seem difficult, but your life purpose helps you see beyond that.

One of the people I like on this topic is Simon Sinek. His book, *Start with Why*, talks about the importance of clarifying "why." His definition is "the purpose or cause; the single driving motivation for action."

He shows this in his diagram, "The Golden Circle."™ On the outside is the "what" of things in your life, the middle ring is the "how," and the bulls-eye is the "why." He equates each of these with different areas of the brain, so the "what" is the cortex (the prefrontal cortex, which is the newest developed part of the brain). The "how" and the "why" are really the limbic area. That's where deep, deep decision-making actually takes place.

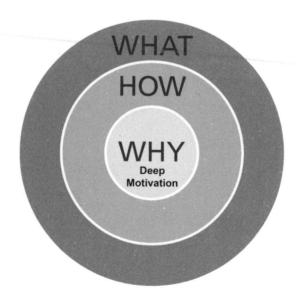

# The Golden Circle

Sinek talks about communicating from the inside out. "When you communicate from the inside out, you are talking directly to the part of the brain that controls behavior and then you allow it to rationalize with tangible things that you say and do. This is from where gut decisions come."

Sinek explains that the biologically-based Golden Circle is a new way of looking at how people approach what they do. "Everyone knows what they do 100 percent. Some know how they do it. Very few people in organizations, in the world, and in their own personal life know *why* they do what they do."

By default, most people define themselves by what they do, such as a dentist, money manager, bricklayer, mom, and so on. By operating from the outside-in, we focus exclusively on the external world, which is ruled by external forces such as friends and family, the media, the Internet, and television. We are bombarded with 24/7 advertising messages telling us something is wrong. We need this car, those clothes, or this pill to make things right.

By connecting our beliefs about who we are to the constantly changing external world, we subject ourselves to enormous stress And we don't get to see who we really are, what our unique life purpose is.

When we choose to operate from our life purpose or our "why," then we shift to an inside-out approach. Connecting to our heart, mind, and intuition moves and inspires us, and the world radically changes for the better. By connecting to our purpose or "why," we become more inspired and we inspire others.

> "To be successful and perform at your highest level, you must commit to living an inside-out life."
> — Steven Griffith

## Framework of the Golden Circle

Success in inspiring others depends upon two core elements:

1. Thinking, communicating, and acting from the inside-out.

2. Finding balance between all three components of the Golden Circle.

In order to be truly successful in achieving the steps above, you must have three things:

**Clarity of WHY:**

This is your purpose, cause, or belief. The "WHY" is the single driving motivation for action.

**Discipline of HOW:**

These are your values or guiding principles. The "HOWs" are the specific actions taken to realize the "WHY."

**Consistency of WHAT:**

The tangible proof or results. "WHATs" are the tangible manifestations of the "WHY."

Inside-out thinking activates the emotional centers of the brain that create unstoppable motivation.[2]

# WHY Are You Here?

Having no established purpose in life is like being on a boat without a rudder.

When clients come to me for High Performance Coaching, one of the very first things we do to get them re-aligned is to determine what their primary purpose is on the planet. I ask them this simple question: "Why are you here?" And the response is pretty much the same every time, "You mean here in your office?"

I respond, "You can answer that or you can also answer just why you're on the planet. Essentially, I want to know what your purpose is. What are your talents and gifts and how are you manifesting them in your everyday life?" Most people look at me like I'm from Mars because they've never taken the time to think about what their purpose is in life.

---

[2] Sinek, Simon, *Start with Why: How Great Leaders Inspire Everyone to Take Action,* Portfolio Trade, 2011.

> "When you are living your true purpose, then extraordinary resources come to your aid and act in alignment with your heart's desire that you can't even imagine."
>
> — Anthony Hopkins,
> Academy Award-winning Actor

We are so stressed out and filled with anxiety from 24/7 connectivity, the constant blitz of media, and the stress of producing, competing and just trying to get through each day that if we don't become still with ourselves, life can pass by without our honoring our true purpose in life. We then rob the world of our true gifts. So, getting to your "why" is really important. This becomes your compass in everything you do.

> "Efforts and courage are not enough without purpose and direction."
>
> — John F. Kennedy

This relates to what we talked about earlier concerning Blind Spots and how they can stop us from seeing our true beliefs and purpose. When we become clear as to what is truly important to us and what our purpose is, we will know what our true values are. When we become present, we now have the ability to strip away all the inauthentic strategies we've created and become who we truly are, not who we were programmed to be. We now have the opportunity to reveal our true gifts.

Following my initial question concerning a person's purpose in life, I ask a few more questions, which you can do to more clearly define your purpose.

- What is really, truly important to you in life?
- What touches, moves, and inspires you?
- What will you get by having this? (Whatever your "why" is.)
- What will you avoid by having your purpose defined?

What I've observed is that when we get connected to our purpose, forces outside of our rational mind come to our aid and enable us to create a road map. This gets us to the next phase of creating our values, which we'll cover in Chapter 6, so that when we know our life purpose, we can create what I call the "values hierarchy" of what's really important to our lives.

When you've done that, you can drill down and get to your goals and be very specific about what you will achieve. You need to know what your values are, e.g., integrity, freedom, love, personal development, money, a great relationship with your family, etc. They become your template for how you make decisions. Your values and life purpose must be in alignment for your ultimate success.

We are all born with a life purpose and when we identify, acknowledge and start working toward our unique purpose, we experience a deeply fulfilled life.

> "To live is to choose. But to choose well, you must know who you are and what you stand for, where you want to go and why you want to get there."
>
> — Kofi Annan, seventh Secretary-General of the United Nations

Another process I use to help my clients find their purpose is Arnold Patent's The Life Purpose Exercise.[3]

Here are the steps:

1. List two of your personal qualities, e.g., *enthusiasm* and *creativity*.

   _____          _____

2. List two ways you enjoy expressing those qualities when interacting with others, e.g., being *supportive* and *inspiring*.

   _____          _____

3. Assume that the world is perfect right now and then imagine what that looks like. How is everyone interacting with everyone else? What does a perfect world feel like, e.g., *harmonious and loving*? Write your answer or statement in the present tense describing the ultimate condition of this perfect world as you see it and remember: A perfect world is a fun place to be.

   _____

   _____

---

[3] Patent, Arnold M., *You Can Have it All: A Simple Guide to a Joyful and Abundant Life* and *The Journey*. www.arnoldpatent.com

4. Combine the three prior answers into a single statement. The example Canfield uses is: "My purpose is to use my enthusiasm and creativity to support and inspire others to freely express their talents in a harmonious and loving way."[4]

_____

_____

Now that you have identified your life purpose, the next important step is to get connected to the "why" of your life purpose. As you now know, when you are emotionally connected to your desires, a strong motivation occurs activating every cell, nerve, and fiber in your body. This accelerates you in a positive direction to manifesting your dreams into reality.

Here is the process: simply ask yourself "Why is this life purpose important to me?" It is important to keep asking yourself the "why" question until you get to the core motivation of your purpose. This can happen quickly, but you must keep asking until you intuitively feel you have reached it. In this process, it is common to recycle previous answers, which is completely normal. By doing this, you're breaking through your subconscious barriers (Blind Spots) to get to your authentic, true motivations.

---

[4] Canfield, Jack, *The Success Principles: How to Get from Where You Are to Where You Want to Be,* Harper, 2005.

Here is my purpose statement, which we will use as an example of how to get to your "why."

> "To use enthusiasm and kindness to support and motivate people to break through from the limitations of their past and move from their high potential to their High Performance in a safe and loving way so they can be *the best they can be* in business and in life."

Here's the process in action:

*Why is my life purpose important to me?*

"So I can feel good about people getting to their next level."

*Why is that important?*

"So they don't have to be in pain from not fully achieving what they want in life."

*Why is that important?*

"So they can have the life they want."

*Why is that important?*

"So they don't have to struggle like I did for so long."

*Why is that important?*

"So I can feel peaceful knowing others are at peace."

*Why is that important?*

"So they don't feel alone in their struggles in life."

*Why is that important?*

"So they feel someone is in their corner."

*Why is that important?*

"So the world is a safer, more peaceful place where people are in harmony with each other while living their true purpose."

This last "why" answer got me to the core of my true motivation. Determining your "why" also applies to specific goals for your life. Every goal we have or everything we want to achieve, we need to know the "why" to ensure our motivation. Here are some examples.

I had a client come in for wellness and health issues that were affecting his business performance. Mike is an entrepreneur in his late forties. He had 20 or 30 pounds of extra body fat and was not in good physical condition.

When he walked in, he said, "I'm having some barriers to losing this extra weight."

*"What's your goal?"* I asked.

"To lose 20 pounds."

*"Why is that important to you?"*

"Well, so I can feel good," he answered.

*"Why is that important to you?"*

"You know, so I can feel healthy."

*"Why is that important to you?"*

"I want to be around for my kids."

*"Why is that important to you?"*

"Because my father passed away when I was 20, and I want to be there for my kids."

I could literally see the shift for him in his eyes. Mike's purpose was not just about losing 20 or 30 pounds and bringing his blood pressure down to get off medication. His "why" for this particular goal was to be present and have an enriched life with his kids. When he realized that, he became highly motivated, he lost all the weight, and got off the medication.

If I had let Mike's purpose be to just lose some weight and he started working out, he would have failed. There would have been no connection to the deep motivational centers of his brain, the area that motivates us to take action. This is why the first step I take with clients is about getting them connected to their purpose and activating their emotions to create fast results.

Another client, Charlie, was the founder of a wellness company. When I worked with him early on in his career, he was really motivated and enthusiastic about helping people, but he had not yet connected to his "why."

So, I asked Charlie why he wanted to help people. He replied, "I want people to be fit and healthy." I asked why that was important to him. He told me about some of his personal struggles and then it all came out when he said, "I saw what my mom went through with her health issues and the pain and suffering it created." His "why" was really to help inspire people to be healthy so they wouldn't have to go through the pain he and his mom experienced. This single process helped him create the internal alignment that motivated him to grow his company into an international success.

I want to make sure you're living your life purpose because there is a direct relationship between working your life purpose, your level of happiness, how you flourish, and creating your ultimate life. That's why the "why" is so integral to the HPC 3-Step System.

Now let's move on to Step 2: Values.

# Chapter 6

# STEP 2 – VALUES

*"Happiness is that state of consciousness which proceeds from the achievement of one's values."*

— Ayn Rand, Novelist, Philosopher, Playwright, and Screenwriter

Step 2 of the HPC 3-Step System covers VALUES, which are essentially our evaluation filters. They are how we decide whether our actions are good or bad, and right or wrong. And they help us decide how we feel about our actions and what's important to us.

The High Performance Pyramid

Have you ever wondered why you are not where you want to be in your business or life, not making the progress you feel you should, not as happy as you want to be, lacking the relationship of your dreams, and/or not making the money you want? You are about to find out if your values are blocking your success.

## Why is it Important to Have a Clear Understanding of What Your Values Are?

The reason why a clear understanding and organization of your values is important is that it creates a solid foundation of the direction and meaning of your life — a blueprint of how you spend your time, money, and energy.

In the absence of your values hierarchy, you become subject to making subconscious, reactive decisions based on the current emotions you're experiencing. This is the number one reason people make poor decisions, underperform, and are misaligned with the true direction of their lives.

By having clear, established values, no matter what situation you find yourself in, you have a clear guide as to how to make conscious decisions that are not distorted by your emotions, which change moment-to-moment, day by day.

Even if our beliefs and purpose are in alignment, but our values aren't clearly established, we will be off track.

Your happiness and performance depend on whether you live according to your values and whether they are aligned with your "why."

To determine your values in any area of your life, ask yourself a simple question. For example: "What is important to me about my life?"

The words that pop into your mind and resonate with you are your values. Words like happiness, career, security, fun, quality relationships, love, creativity, and accomplishment might be your values.

If you ask what is important about your health, you might use words like energy, stamina, longevity, and looking good.

For myself, one of my top five values is personal development. Personal development is very high on my personal values list. If I'm not reading, researching, seeking out tools and helping others, I'm not really fulfilling my life purpose or expanding myself. I'm not living my values.

## Values Provide Motivation

What motivates you to achieve or be happy are your values. Before you do anything in life, your values motivate and determine how you spend your time, energy, and money.

Values determine how you feel about what you have done, and how you feel about yourself and others.

Here are the steps to determine your values.

1. Ask yourself this question: "What is most important about who I am in the world?"

   Try to keep your answer as brief as possible, ideally to one or two words. (Using your own words and not the answers others have used about you is important when listing your values. The list needs to be all about you, not them.)

2. Prioritize your answers in order from most important to least important for however many you've listed, like the following example:

No. 1   Health & Wellness          No. 4   Friendship

No. 2   Money                      No. 5   Integrity

No. 3   Love                       No. 6   Career

3. Now for the "truth" question. Ask yourself: "If I could have my MOST IMPORTANT answer (No. 1), but NOT HAVE No. 2, would that be ok?"

If the answer is YES, then you have the order correct. But if your answer is NO, then swap the priority in your hierarchy around, making No. 2 No. 1.

Continue asking this question with each answer on your list, for example: "If I could have answer No. 1, BUT NOT No. 3, would that be ok?"

Repeat this entire exercise beginning with answer No. 2 until that value has been compared to all the values below it. Repeat this with value No. 3 and those answers below it and so on.

You may find that you have to really take some time to think about the answers. By doing this, it can provide you with some very valuable information. Take note of how you feel about each one, and the choices that cause you difficulty.

Are there any conflicts in your priorities?

You might be surprised to discover that the values you thought were important to you are not actually as high up on your list as you initially considered them.

For instance, you may have thought that Friendship was important to you, and often felt guilty that you did not stay in touch with your friends on a frequent basis. In doing this exercise, you may find that in fact Friendship is not as high on your list as Integrity. In this case, there is a conflict between the two that you will need to resolve.

Importantly, this values alignment process — what is most important to you — can be applied to any area of your life. (At the end of this section, you'll have a chance to align you values in life, career, relationships, health and wellness, personal development, and fun and recreation.)

A few more questions to think about in relationship to your "why." Review your list, and ask yourself the following questions:

1. What do my values need to be in order to be aligned with who I am?

2. Do I need to add any other values to the list or eliminate any?

3. What do my values need to be in order for me to be all that I can be?

4. What benefits do I get from having this particular value in this position in my values hierarchy?

Are the values in your life still appropriate for the person you've become? You may be carrying a value from your past, from your parents, or previous circumstances that are no longer of any use or benefit to you. So, be open to questioning the usefulness of your values, and if a value has no benefit, get rid of it or replace it with a more useful value.

In my High Performance Coaching, establishing what your values are is a very important step. This is because you can figure out your life purpose and your "why," but if your values are off, you are not going to get there because you will be making decisions that conflict with each other.

As an example of how powerful values are, I was working with one of my clients, Mark MacDonald early in his career. Mark is a nutrition coach to the stars, New York Times bestselling author of *Body Confidence* and *Why Kids Make You Fat*, founder of Venice Nutrition, and just an extraordinary human being.

We sat down to review his values and one of the first things we found out was that for him, family came first. His business was second, his wellness third, and fun and recreation were fourth. I then started asking him some questions.

*"I see family is first,"* I stated.

"Yes," he replied, "my wife is my first priority."

Then I asked, *"If your business is failing because you are not putting enough time into it, as long as you have a good relationship with your wife, is that OK?"*

"No, that would be horrible. I wouldn't be fulfilling my life purpose or be able to satisfy my financial obligations. I'd be worried about working and not making enough money," Mark responded.

*"You have a values conflict,"* I told him. *"I know your wife is very important, however, if you put your wife before your business and your health, you are going to be deeply unhappy and she is not going to feel very good either."*

Mark re-aligned his values. His first value became mental and physical health, and having a successful business became his second value.

*"Mark, when your health and wellness and your business are performing at a high level, your wife will feel she's #1. If your health and your business are not doing well, she will not,"* I stated succinctly.

Mark got it, shifted his values, and focused on his business. This gave him more freedom to really pursue his business and also connect more deeply with his wife. Mark now has about five hundred nutrition centers worldwide, his own nutritional product line, is a regular contributor on CNN, has his own wellness segment on the HLN network, and is a New York Times best-selling author. Re-aligning his values gave him the freedom to connect more deeply with his family and simultaneously live his dream.

To re-align your values, just ask yourself the simple question: "What is important to me about my life?" Make a list of your answers and keep asking the question, "What's important to me about who I am?" Record your answers.

After you've written down seven to ten answers, prioritize the first five and go through the simple process of prioritizing what we went over earlier to make sure your values are in alignment.

For example, if your number one value is having freedom in your life, and you take that to mean working only 20 hours a week, and your second priority is to retire by the time you're 35 and you're currently 30 years old, unless you make more per hour than 99 percent of America, you have a conflict.

The conflict Mark had was that in his mind's eye his wife was first, which is common. What was happening is that he wasn't fully engaging in his business. While he was successful, he was not where he wanted to be and not accelerating his business at the speed he wanted because he was in a fundamental values conflict.

Once your values are in alignment, the second step in the 3-Step HPC System, you now have a guide to where you invest your time, money, energy, who you spend time with, and the quality of the relationships you have.

The following pages are created for you to align your top five values in the following areas: life, business/career, relationships, health and wellness, personal development, and fun and recreation.

# Aligning Your Values

What's important to me in my life?

| Answer | Priority # |
| --- | --- |
| | |
| | |
| | |
| | |
| | |
| | |
| | |
| | |
| | |
| | |
| | |

# What's important to me in my business/career?

| Answer | Priority # |
|--------|-----------|
|        |           |
|        |           |
|        |           |
|        |           |
|        |           |
|        |           |
|        |           |
|        |           |
|        |           |
|        |           |
|        |           |

## What's important to me in my relationships?

| Answer | Priority # |
| --- | --- |
| | |
| | |
| | |
| | |
| | |
| | |
| | |
| | |
| | |
| | |
| | |

# What's important to me for my health and wellness?

| Answer | Priority # |
| --- | --- |
| | |
| | |
| | |
| | |
| | |
| | |
| | |
| | |
| | |
| | |
| | |

# What's important to me for my personal development?

| Answer | Priority # |
|---|---|
| _____ | _____ |
| _____ | _____ |
| _____ | _____ |
| _____ | _____ |
| _____ | _____ |
| _____ | _____ |
| _____ | _____ |
| _____ | _____ |
| _____ | _____ |
| _____ | _____ |
| _____ | _____ |
| _____ | _____ |

# What's important for me for fun and recreation?

| Answer | Priority # |
| --- | --- |
| | |
| | |
| | |
| | |
| | |
| | |
| | |
| | |
| | |
| | |
| | |

You are now over halfway through the HPC 3-Step System for you to perform at your very best. You have completed the first step of aligning your beliefs and identifying your Blind Spot. You have defined your life purpose and "why," your values are now aligned, and now it is time for Step 3: Communication.

# Chapter 7

# STEP 3 – COMMUNICATION

*"We don't see things as they are, we see things as we are."*

— Anaïs Nin, Author

The High Performance Pyramid

Step 3 in my HPC System is COMMUNICATION. How effectively you can focus in a positive way on your internal self-talk, regulate your emotions and how you speak in the world, will determine your success. In the next two chapters, we will cover how to maximize your mental and emotional patterns to perform at your highest performance state.

Your beliefs, values, goals, and life purpose are what you have programmed by the continuous thoughts, feelings and language you use, and subsequent actions you take. When the positive outweighs the negative, you flourish. When that is reversed, you get depressed, stressed out, ultimately disconnected from your true purpose in life, and you underperform.

Imagine that your subconscious is recording everything you're feeling and saying. Most of us are not even aware that this process is taking place — unaware of what is being recorded, what we are saying to ourselves, and often what we are saying out in the world. Those thoughts and emotions are either working for us to help us achieve our goals by supporting our beliefs, values and life purpose, or they are working against us.

My ultimate goal for you with this book, the same as when I work with CEOs, executives, entrepreneurs, celebrities, athletes and entertainment professionals, is to help train your thoughts, emotions, and communication to use in a High Performance way to get what you want.

> "Communication is an exchange of energy and information."
> — Dan Siegel, Founder,
> Interpersonal Neurobiology

## Internal Communication

Communication activates your beliefs, values, your purpose, and your goals. When they are aligned and your internal communication and emotional state are at a positive high level, you are a high-performance engine running on all cylinders.

The right communication skills put your life on the fast track to High Performance.

Many times, our minds will create random thoughts and emotions. We cannot always predict when or what emotions will appear. At the end of the day, how we interpret our emotions and thoughts is what counts, not what the thoughts and emotions were. That is the big difference. If we can have the correct interpretation of our thoughts and emotions and have the tools to shift them, we will succeed.

# Mindfulness

One of the greatest tools in my High Performance System is "mindfulness" and the use of meditation and other mindfulness tools to regulate our mental and emotional states. By definition, as you learned earlier, mindfulness is that state of "present moment awareness without judgment." In simple terms, when you are in the flow and in direct experience. By practicing being in the moment, you begin to live a life that responds to events rationally rather than reacting emotionally.

This first mindfulness technique of meditating is really just sitting quietly and focusing on a neutral spot on your body. Use the breath from the diaphragm, right by the belly button. Just notice the diaphragm rising and falling.

Sit comfortably, in an upright position, with your eyes closed. Notice your breath without trying to get into any state. This is a moment-to-moment awareness without any judgment for whatever happens.

When you begin, you may have a lot of thoughts roaming around in your head and this can be overwhelming. You are not trying to reach any kind of particular state, but instead letting the thoughts and feelings come up and identifying them for what they are, as you focus on your breathing.

> "When we are mindful, deeply in touch with the present moment, our understanding of what is going on deepens, and we begin to be filled with acceptance, joy, peace, and love."
>
> — Thich Nhat Hanh,
> Buddhist Monk and Author

When a thought comes, just be with it for a moment, label it as a thought, then go back to focusing on your breathing.

Feeling sad, excited, confused, cautious? That's okay. Be with that for a moment and label it as an emotion. Come back to your breathing and focusing on your diaphragm.

This meditative practice helps you simply "identify" or acknowledge what's coming up in your mind rather than reacting. It builds the core supportive structure in your mind's eye for you to be present and mindful when life is coming at you.

During meditation, as thoughts and feelings arise, the goal is to just label them as a thought or feeling. The challenge in all meditation many times is that we get caught up by those thoughts and feelings.

> "It's all about returning to your breath without judging or reacting to the thoughts and emotions you're experiencing."
> — Steven Griffith

Another top researcher whose findings support the mindfulness approach is Matthew Lieberman at UCLA, who through his research discovered that the simple act of identifying emotions helps the brain regulate them. It has been found that when individuals took the time to identify the emotions they were experiencing, e.g., anger, sadness, upset and so on, and didn't focus on them just identified them, they felt better and performed better. That's what we do in mindfulness and why it's so important. This translates to less distraction, more focus, and higher levels of performance.

The more we practice the mindfulness way of being, the less reactive we become. It helps us create new neural connections in our brains, which helps us identify what is really going on with our thoughts and emotions and create an environment where we are truly present. This is the benefit when we sit in meditation — mindfulness.

We begin to learn to experience our thoughts and feelings without reacting. Our direct experience is "I'm totally present with myself." When we're totally present with our bodies, we have full access to our five senses, full cognitive abilities and complete creativity, which we are biologically designed to be in and experience.

Have you ever been deeply in conversation? You have that intense rapport with a friend or lover, and you're just deeply connecting. You are not thinking *about* the conversation, you're *in* the conversation.

In similar fashion, this could occur when you're singing your favorite song, playing your favorite sport, dancing to your favorite music, when you're completely present and in full enjoyment of the experience — it's the state of no thoughts, just being.

When we're totally present, we have the "direct experience" of life. For instance, it's the middle of the summer and you're sitting on a dock by the ocean — you're feeling the warm sun on your face, enjoying the breeze and view of the ocean, smelling the fresh ocean air, and listening to the seagulls — you're being present.

Compare this to sitting on the dock by the ocean and all you're thinking about is: "Did I turn the stove off?" "Why are my kids being so difficult?" "I can't remember if I sent that e-mail." "Am I going to get that promotion?" For most of us, this "narrative state" is how we're living day to day — thinking about what we're doing, having a constant internal dialogue. This is a state that creates stress and anxiety.

When we're in our narrative, our ability to fully access all of our senses is diminished. Our cognitive ability, our actual thinking processes, is diminished, as well as our ability to handle stress. Our stress and/or anxiety rises and our happiness level goes down.

## Present, Pause & Proceed™

To counteract this narrative state and to help you operate rationally when you have an argument, a disappointment, things don't go your way, you get triggered emotionally and to perform at your highest level, I created the mindfulness performance technique called Present, Pause, and Proceed,™ using ancient wisdom techniques to get modern results in today's high-paced, 24/7 connected world.

My clients have reported that this technique has helped them regulate stressful situations, make better decisions, and perform at their optimal level under pressure. It teaches someone to be mindful: **Present** to their mental and emotional state and what's happening for them in the moment, **Pause** to think rationally and evaluate ("What do I want to do or not do?"), and then **Proceed** into the world with a mindful High Performance strategy.

- Step 1: Notice the physical sensations occurring in your body, e.g., chest, throat, stomach, etc. Once identified, take a deep, diaphragmatic breath and exhale.

- Step 2: Move up into your head and distinguish the emotions from the sensations. Then identify and label them as: I'm frustrated, I'm angry, I'm anxious, I'm sad, etc.

- Step 3: Take another diaphragmatic breath. Then ask yourself, "What do I have that I don't want?" or "What don't I have that I want?" Next, take the appropriate actions that are in alignment with what you want. By using this mindfulness technique, you immediately short circuit the old, subconscious emotional reactive system and immediately create new, positive results. You are then able to act in your best interests knowing your purpose and that's the model of the Present, Pause, & Proceed technique.

When you use this technique, your whole world changes. This is what high performers do. They think rationally in all conditions. They respond rather than react, which creates High Performance.

I recently taught the Present, Pause, & Proceed technique to a client of mine, Bob, a VP of Sales at an advertising company.

Bob told me, "I was in a meeting. I was having this intense, pounding sensation in my head, and I just recognized right there that I should not react."

Bob took a deep breath and identified his feelings and he realized that, "Man, I'm really pissed off. I'm angry, I'm frustrated." Then he asked himself, "What do I want in this situation? I want to put this conversation off until tomorrow and I want to talk about how I can increase sales for the company."

Taking another deep breath, Bob said to the CEO, "I'm really sensing frustration from both of us. What I want is for us to have a successful conversation and I feel like it's not going in that direction. Can we complete this conversation when we're both more grounded? How's tomorrow morning at 9?"

Instead of blowing up and needing to have multiple conversations to repair their unproductive conversation, or even possibly getting fired, Bob used mindfulness and became present to the sensations in his body — the emotions — moved up into his head, determined rationally what emotions he was having, thought about what he wanted, and then communicated in a responsive way that created a positive outcome.

By using the Present, Pause, & Proceed mindfulness technique, we don't shut emotions down, we in fact experience them more deeply and respond instead of unconsciously react.

When we identify our feelings and say, "I'm mad, sad, glad, happy, frustrated, angry," or whatever emotion we are having, the area of our brain that helps regulate our emotions is activated.

This cognitive step affects our physiology, our brain starts helping us, and we become more present to how best to move forward. We replace reacting with responding — still feeling the emotions, still being passionate and engaged with our lives, but not letting our emotions work against us. Instead, letting them work for us.

## Mindfulness Meditation

Here is another tool to cultivate mindfulness (mindful meditation), which I suggest you do daily from 5 - 20 minutes:

Begin by closing your eyes, sitting upright in a comfortable position, focusing on your diaphragm (by your belly button), and notice the diaphragm rising and falling as you breathe naturally. As you focus on your diaphragm, breathing naturally, remember that this technique is not to get into any particular state or any way of being. It's really about moment-to-moment awareness with whatever happens without any judgments.

As you sit in this process of meditation, it is natural for emotions and thoughts to arise. Just be with them for a moment and identify them as a thought or emotion and then come back to your breath at your diaphragm.

It's not about staying in a Zen state, it's actually quite different. It's all about being with what is in the moment, identifying it, and returning to your breath.

Practicing this meditation technique, as well as the Present, Pause, & Proceed technique, you will begin to focus on the here and now and not the past or future. This will help you step away from your distractive thinking, and allow you to proceed in a more balanced state where you are no longer emotionally reactive, and instead responding rationally.

As a bonus gift to you, to create momentum and get you started in creating positive results, I've included this audio link to guide you through the meditation process:

**For a free, guided meditation:**
**http://www.stevengriffith.com/free-meditation/**

## Head – Heart – Body

Another mindfulness technique to increase your performance that I adapted and added to is called Head-Heart-Body from Pamela Weiss, a mindfulness educator.

One of the biggest challenges today is making the right, decisive decisions and taking actions that are aligned with your beliefs, values, and purpose. This technique is designed for you to go quickly and easily within and get centered so you can move forward with the right intention and strategies to perform at your highest level. If you are leading, managing, selling, negotiating, relationship building or navigating your personal life, becoming present in the moment and knowing what your internal state is will give you the insight on how to proceed.

Step One — Begin by sitting comfortably with eyes open or closed, take one deep breath in, and exhale letting your body settle in and relax. Bring your attention to your Head and notice what thoughts you're having, what you're picturing, and what you're remembering or reviewing in the moment right now.

- Are you worrying?
- Are you judging?
- Are you anticipating?

Just observe whatever it is without any judgment or trying to change what is appearing. This is all about noticing your mental patterns. Just notice your thoughts, what you're reviewing, what you're mentally focusing on. Just be with whatever appears. (1-2min)

Step Two — Bring your attention down to your chest to the Heart center and take a deep breath in and exhale. As you turn your attention to your Heart, notice what feelings or emotions you're having.

- What is your mood or attitude?
- Are you frustrated, excited, happy, bored, content?

Once again, there's no right or wrong way of being. Just notice in this moment what your feelings are. What attitude is present, what is your mood? You don't need to shift, change, or alter anything — just be present to what is. Without judging anything, just invite the feelings in.

Step Three — Now move into your Body. Take a breath in and exhale and move your attention to your diaphragm. Just notice your belly rising and falling, and as you notice your belly rising and falling, observe what's happening in your Body.

- Is there tension or relaxation?
- Is there warmth or coolness?
- Is there pain or fatigue?

Just invite your Body to express itself, and as you've done in the two previous centers, notice without any judgment, without any fixing or changing, but simply scanning your Body to see what is. Just notice what is.

I've created a fourth step and added it to Weiss's framework. It's a valuable tool to move internal wisdom into action. Step Four — Visualize your Head, Heart, and Body centers connected, communicating with each other, and ask yourself internally, "What do I need to know right now?" Just sit for a minute or so being present to the wisdom of your complete self and take notice of whatever internal messages come forward.

By utilizing the Head – Heart – Body technique, you can internally listen to and fully evaluate what state you're in. You can now make conscious decisions of what to do or not do in your business or personal life. This allows you to avoid being emotionally hijacked, doing things that will not ultimately serve you, and take actions and make decisions that are in alignment with what you truly want in life!

> ## "The more present you are, the higher you perform in business and life."
> — Steven Griffith

## Negative Thoughts & Feelings and How to Turn Them Around

World famous psychiatrist, Dr. Daniel Amen of the Amen Clinic, has written many books on the brain and human behavior. His theory of ANTs (Automatic Negative Thoughts) is that we're going to have automatic negative thoughts and these thoughts are not what matters. How we interpret these thoughts is what counts.

We cannot always control what thoughts and feelings arise, but we absolutely can control what we do with them. This is part of High Performance Coaching. Our old programming often dictates our thoughts and feelings and how we react to them — old programming from mom and dad, negative life events, and so on where we started believing these untrue and limiting beliefs about ourselves. What you now know is called your Blind Spot.

You've already identified what your Blind Spot is by going through the HPC System, creating new awareness and strategies to break out of it by consciously regulating your thoughts, emotions, and language.

> "The thoughts that go through your mind moment by moment have a significant impact on how your brain works."
> — Dr. Daniel Amen, Psychiatrist and Author, *Change Your Brain, Change Your Life*

This leads me to two fantastic researchers. UCLA professors Jeffrey Schwartz and Rebecca Gladding, authors of *You Are Not Your Brain*, are experts in deceptive brain messages. I have adapted their 4-step process based on mindfulness and cognitive conditioning into the High Performance Coaching System. In their book, they state:

"We believe that the mind is intimately connected with and can exert powerful effects on the brain. In short, we believe that people are so much more than what their brain is trying to tell them they are, and that the brain often gets in the way of their long-term goals and values in life, their true self."

Schwartz and Gladding believe "We have the ability to harness the power of focused attention to change our brains in ways that are healthy and beneficial to us. Even more to the point, many of the thoughts, impulses, urges, and sensations we experience do not reflect who we really are in life. These are false missives and are not true representations of us, but rather inaccurate, highly-deceptive brain messages." These messages are derived from old conditioning that aren't true and that we've carried around with us for many, many years.

"Old wiring creates anxiety, self-doubt, perfectionism, behaving in ways or engaging in habits that are not good for us, over-texting, over-analyzing, stress eating, drinking too much, and so on, ignoring our true self, and wholeheartedly believing the stream of negative thoughts coursing through your head."

Here are the steps I've adapted and re-formulated to turn negative thoughts and emotions around for positive results:

**Step 1: Recognize.** Recognize you are having deceptive brain messages, e.g., any unhelpful thoughts, urges, desires and impulses, followed by identifying the uncomfortable sensations/emotions, and then calling them what they are. So, in Step 1, we really want to recognize, "There's something coming at me that I know is deceptive. Wow, I'm upset, I'm angry, I'm frustrated." Next, in the process, take three deep 4-7-8 diaphragmatic breaths (this breath technique is covered in Chapter 9).

By identifying and breathing, this helps your brain and body regulate your emotions and get ahold of the situation.

**Step 2: Re-frame.** Alter your perception of the significance of the deceptive brain message. By saying, "These urges, desires, and impulses are not really me…they are my brain trying to trick me into believing they are me. They are just my brain and I can change that." In that re-framing process, also add, "Is this impulse helping or hurting me? This is really not me. It's an old pattern, an old belief."

Identify that this old pattern is running you, instead of you running yourself.

**Step 3: Re-condition.** Focus your attention on a positive activity (see Chapter 9 tools: Breathing, Visualization, Spinning, etc.) even while the false and negative deceptive messages are still present and bothering you. This is really important: You have to truly hear and understand that during this shift you are re-conditioning your nervous system. It may actually not feel very good at first. You must take the actions first and then the positive emotions will follow in time. This step is the most important in this process for creating new, lasting, and positive behaviors.

**Step 4: Re-Integrate.** This step is about integrating the three previous steps and bringing in a higher sense of self. By being consciously aware of the process you're in and having an internal dialogue with yourself, you will re-integrate and solidify your new behaviors and thoughts. As you assess the previous three steps, you'll begin to clearly see the thoughts, urges, and impulses that were just sensations based on deceptive brain messages. They are not you and you can take control of them!

Here's a quick story that demonstrates this 4-step process in action. A sales executive I coached, Sophia, is in the entertainment industry and was struggling with texting and constantly checking her e-mail. She felt she had to check her e-mail every five minutes or else she'd miss out on something. She had to be in constant connection. Sound familiar to you?

First, we worked together to identify that in reality, checking e-mails every five minutes was not productive and if there were something urgent, people would call.

**Step 1** for Sophia, **Recognize,** was to identify the trigger: "I'm having this urge to check my e-mail. I need to check it right now." These impulses were deceptive brain messages. Next, was identifying the sensations and feelings attached to the thoughts. She labeled them as "I am anxious" and "I am stressed." She next took three 4-7-8 breaths and went on to Step 2.

**Step 2, Re-frame.** Sophia reminded herself why this was bothering her. She then said to herself: "I'm having an urge to check my e-mail because it gives me a rush when there's something in the inbox. It feels good." She continued, "I am not my brain. I do not have to respond to every impulse, and there's nothing that important in my inbox that can't wait."

**Step 3, Re-condition.** While still having anxiety, Sophia chose to step into her Circle of Excellence (Chapter 9) and visualized a calm state, which began to distract and re-condition her brain.

**Step 4, Re-integrate.** Sophia brought her higher sense of self forward, dialogued with herself, and recognized that the urge to check e-mail is nothing more than a feeling of deceptive brain messages. It's not something that needs to be taken seriously and paid attention to. In fact, giving into this urge just makes the underlying brain circuitry — the wiring — stronger.

The more she checked her e-mail, the more frequently and intense the urges became. So, she dismissed the deceptive brain messages and instead did something healthy and productive utilizing the 4 Steps.

# High Performance Language
## to Get What You Want

As you master your ability to regulate and focus your mental and emotional patterns to get what you want and perform at your highest level, it's just as important to communicate and use language to support your positive state.

The language we use and how we communicate sends a signal to ourselves and others that supports our beliefs, values, purpose, and goals — or holds us back.

On the next two pages are positive words to use to replace your old disempowering ones. By using these new words in your conversations, both personally and professionally, you will create communications that are congruent and that achieve the rapid results you want in your life.

# Positive Replacement Words

| Change | Maybe | to | Yes, no, I will consider |
|--------|-------|-----|--------------------------|
| Change | Try | to | I will |
| Change | Problem | to | Challenge |
| Change | Probably | to | Yes, no, I will or will not |
| Change | I should | to | I will |
| Change | Kind of | to | It is or it isn't |
| Change | You make me | to | I choose or I create for myself |
| Change | Will you? | to | My request is |
| Change | I don't know | to | I choose to know, I'll find out |
| Change | It's hard | to | It's a challenge |
| Change | I need | to | I desire… or I choose… |
| Change | I'm not | to | I am |
| Change | Let me | to | I desire... or I choose... |
| Change | It's like | to | It is or it isn't |
| Change | I think so | to | I know |
| Change | I want | to | My choice is, I require… |
| Change | I must | to | I will, I choose |
| Change | I hope | to | My choice is… |
| Change | I've got to | to | I choose to |

| | | | |
|---|---|---|---|
| Change | Almost | to | It is or it isn't |
| Change | Decide | to | My choice is… |
| Change | I would | to | I will |
| Change | I could | to | I can |
| Change | I wish | to | I choose to |
| Change | If all else fails | to | My highest choice is… |
| Change | At least | to | At most |
| Change | Doesn't it? | to | Does it? |
| Change | Can't you? | to | Can you? |
| Change | Perhaps | to | I will, I choose |
| Change | But | to | And |

As we use these words, when we're thinking and speaking, we are causing changes in our emotional state that either support our goals or detract from them. We're either going towards our goals or away from them — we are either moving towards the life we want or away from it.

By regulating your internal state and using this new language on a regular basis along with the HPC System, you begin to accelerate the positive results you want in business and in life.

# Chapter 8

# GOALS

*"Our goals can only be reached
through a vehicle of a plan, in which
we must fervently believe, and upon
which we must vigorously act.
There is no other route to success."*

— Pablo Picasso, Artist

You now have the knowledge and understanding of the HPC 3-Step System for aligning your beliefs, values, and communication with your life purpose. Now it's time to take that alignment and actualize it in a concrete way that gets you what you want. How you attain what you want in life is a very simple formula once you're internally aligned and that's by identifying what you specifically want through goals. Going through the HPC System and not setting goals will revert you back to and keep you enmeshed in your old Blind Spots. Setting goals and activating new strategies and actions will consistently break the patterns of your Blind Spots from the past and create new, neural connections that will accelerate you to your next level of business and personal High Performance.

Goal setting is a powerful process for thinking about your ideal future, and for motivating yourself to turn your vision of this future into reality. By knowing precisely what you want to achieve, you know where you have to concentrate your efforts.

## Why Set Goals?

Goal setting is used by top-athletes, successful executives, entrepreneurs, entertainment professionals, and high performers in all fields.

Goal setting focuses your acquisition of knowledge, and helps you to organize your time and your resources so that you can make the very most of your life.

> "Setting goals gives you long-term vision and short-term 'motivation.'"

> "If you don't design your life, someone else will and it could get ugly."
>
> — Anonymous

By setting clearly-defined goals, you can measure and take pride in the achievement of those goals, and you'll see forward progress in what might previously have seemed a long, pointless grind. You will also raise your self-confidence as you recognize your own ability and competence in achieving the goals you've set.

I'm sure you've heard this advice before: "Write your goals down." In today's fast-paced world where multitasking is the norm 24/7, the more we write down our goals the greater our ability to put our focused attention on what's important and achieve what we truly desire. When you write things down, a chain of events is set in motion that will change your life.

Having our goals on paper gives us more cognitive functioning, creativity, and energy to achieve our goals and a greater capacity in our minds.

> "People with clear, written goals, accomplish far more in a shorter period of time than people without them could ever imagine."
>
> — Brian Tracy, Author and Motivational Speaker

We set goals for one simple reason: to facilitate and allow ourselves the chance to actualize what we want. HPC's primary focus is to aid you in achieving your desires as quickly as possible.

## Goal Setting Questions

- What is my goal/outcome?

- Where am I today?

- What resources do I already have to obtain my goal?

- What resources will I have to get? What will I need? (people/things)

- What is the time frame?

- How will I know when I have it?

- Have I ever done it before?

- What will I gain or lose when I get it?

- What will it allow me to have or do when I have it?

- What tangible things will I have in my life when I have this goal, and how will it impact me and the people in my life?

# Setting SMART Goals

SMART means the goal must be:

Specific: Create your goals with as much detail as possible (who, what, where, when, and why).

Measurable: Establish specific criteria for measuring your goals. Answer the question: How will I know when it is accomplished? This will give you the details for how to measure it.

Attainable: Appropriate and inspired actions to take to create your desired goals.

Realistic: Goals that you are both *willing* and *able* to put the appropriate effort into and that represent substantial progress toward stretching you just enough.

Time-certain: Scheduled and trackable tasks and timelines. This creates a sense of urgency that inspires action.

# Success Begins with Visualizing Results

> "To accomplish great things, we must first dream, then visualize, then plan... believe...act!"
> — Alfred A. Montapert, American Author

Michelangelo said this about his statue of David: "I saw the angel in the marble and carved until I set him free." This remark suggests that Michelangelo's mental imagery allowed him to birth a genius creation from his subconscious mind.

The subconscious mind does not know the difference between fantasy and reality. In the process of visualizing, imagining you're in that state of High Performance for a specific goal you want, seeing what you see, hearing what you hear, and feeling what you feel as if you're in that moment right now — the subconscious mind takes the visualization as reality and programs its outcome for that. This is why top Olympic and professional athletes all use visualization to perform at their highest level.

Scientist, David R. Hamilton, PhD, author of *How Your Mind Can Heal Your Body*, has studied the mind-body connection and says in his latest book, *It's the Thought that Counts: Why Mind Over Matter Really Works*, that thoughts, feelings, and intentions are strong enough to affect a human's genes.

In his article, "Visualization Alters the Brain," Dr. Hamilton says, "Visualization techniques, for instance, are regularly used by thousands of people and have often produced what may be seen as nothing short of miracles. ...Your brain cannot tell the difference between something that's real and whether you are just imagining it."

In a Harvard Medical School study done in 1994, two sets of volunteers learned a simple five-fingered combination of notes. One group practiced the notes for two hours a day, every day, for five consecutive days on a real piano. The other group practiced the same exercise every day for two hours a day, also for five consecutive days, but without a piano and just visualized they were playing a piano and hearing the notes. After the five days had been completed, brain scans were taken of each group. Remarkably, the "maps" of each group's brains had grown the same amount. This clearly showed that our brains cannot distinguish between real and imagined scenarios.

## Meditate on the Conditions You Wish to Produce

Dr. Wayne Dyer, internationally renowned author and speaker in the field of self-development, in his book, *The Power of Intention: Learning to Co-create Your World Your Way,* says to "continuously contemplate yourself as being surrounded by the conditions you wish to produce." He illustrates this idea by saying that the Wright brothers didn't contemplate staying on the ground just as Thomas Edison didn't contemplate a world without light.

> "Visualize this thing that you want, see it, feel it, believe in it. Make your mental blueprint, and begin to build."
> — Robert Collier, American Author

## Visualization Success Strategies

Visualizing a result is key in achieving any business or personal goal. Here are a couple of visualization techniques I use with my clients that you'll find very beneficial.

*Practice a visualization meditation* — As regularly as possible, find a quiet, relaxing place to meditate on a goal or desired outcome. First, clear your mind and become present, not thinking about anything, but where you are right now. As you become more relaxed, visualize the desired positive outcome taking in all the details and using your five senses to experience even more intently what you desire as if it's already happening now.

Then, throughout your day, be conscious of the clues that may appear as the goal is being manifested, such as a surprise phone call, a relevant book comes your way, something is said in conversation, etc. This information will help lead you to the results you desire.

*Create a vision board* — Vision boards add clarity and more deeply imprint dreams and goals on the mind. On a poster board of any size, paste pictures, symbols, words from magazines, and other sources onto the board. Use creativity and intention, and think about all you desire in business and in life from, say, that vacation in Italy to the completion of a longstanding project. Keep this board in a place where you can spend time visualizing it daily.

It's important to create a vision of what you truly want and release the constraints of what you think you feel you need. By clearly identifying what you truly want versus what you need, you will help yourself break free of your old limiting beliefs about what you can or cannot have in your life.

Visualizing how life can really be — free of your Blind Spot — is key to achieving goals and, most importantly, to creating a life by design rather than by accident, by your past conditioning, or by someone else's agenda.

The following pages give you an opportunity to write down your goals for business/career, finances, personal development, wellness, relationships, things you desire, and way of being (kind, compassionate, patient, etc.).

# Goal Setting

Write Out Five Business/Career Goals

1. _____

2. _____

3. _____

4. _____

5. _____


Write Out Five Financial Goals

1. _____

2. _____

3. _____

4. _____

5. _____

## Write Out Five Personal Development Goals

1. _____

2. _____

3. _____

4. _____

5. _____


## Write Out Five Wellness Goals

1. _____

2. _____

3. _____

4. _____

5. _____

Write Out Five Relationship Goals

1. _____

2. _____

3. _____

4. _____

5. _____


Write Out Five "Things" Goals e.g., house, car, clothes, etc.

1. _____

2. _____

3. _____

4. _____

5. _____

Write Out Five "Way of Being" Goals, e.g., kind, compassionate, patient, etc.

1. _____

2. _____

3. _____

4. _____

5. _____

> "To truly reach your goals, you must ask yourself one simple question: Who do I need to be to have what I want?"
>
> — Steven Griffith

# Chapter 9

# HOW TO
# SHIFT TO YOUR
# HIGH PERFORMANCE
# STATE

*"Some people want it to happen,
some wish it would happen,
others make it happen."*

— Michael Jordan, NBA Hall of Famer

The HPC 3-Step System is designed to create and maintain your High Performance state and program mental/emotional patterns for your success. With today's competitive, high-pressured, unpredictable and non-stop world, most people are filled with stress, anxiety, a sense of overwhelm and fear, and are easily distracted and taken off course. The more you can maintain Your High Performance state, the more successful you will be!

If you're pushing yourself to perform at your highest level, you need to be able to consciously respond quickly and effectively and be at your best. That's High Performance.

## Seven Tools for Success

The following are seven powerful tools I have used with thousands of people with great success. Using them, you can easily shift negative states, maintain positive ones and maximize High Performance to be more physically relaxed, mentally alert, emotionally calm, and completely present and performing at your best.

1. Breathing
2. Circle of Excellence
3. Spinning
4. Visualization
5. Gratitude
6. Laughter
7. Hypnosis

# 1. BREATHING

One of the best tools to instantly reduce stress and anxiety is breathing. How many times have you heard, "Take a deep breath" when facing a tense situation or when trying to clear your mind and relax? There's a reason: Consciously breathing causes a number of things to happen for us from helping our mind relax momentarily to giving our bodies a break by introducing more oxygen into our bloodstreams.

Breathing, which is integral to our ability to be alive, is overlooked by most of us since we do it automatically. If you think about it, though, each minute of our future is dependent on our next breath.

> "If I had to limit my advice on healthier living to just one tip, it would be simply to learn how to breathe correctly."
> — Dr. Andrew Weil, Physician and Author, *Natural Health, Natural Medicine*

That's how important breathing is. It not only sustains us by infusing our bodies with much-needed oxygen, but it's also key in maintaining an overall healthy body and an alert mind.

Dr. Weil, one of the leading wellness experts in the world and founder and director of the Arizona Center for Integrative Medicine, explains in his work that each breath positively impacts our entire physiological system from increasing our energy, to lowering blood pressure, improving circulation, and mitigating anxiety disorders without drug intervention.

As you know, breathing is both automatic and voluntary. Most importantly, we can regulate our breathing for things like meditation. It's highly beneficial as you take mastery of your life and achieve your goals and dreams.

I have taught this technique to many of my clients and they have told me they've experienced a tremendous reduction in stress and anxiety resulting in peace, clear headedness, greater focus, and Higher Performance.

## The 4-7-8 (Relaxing Breath) Exercise

This is one of the simplest exercises you can do that doesn't require a lot of time, equipment, a special place or time to do it, or take a lot of effort. In fact, it is one of the fastest ways to reduce your anxiety, stress, and physical tension.

Sitting up straight in a chair, close your eyes and just breath gently, letting your body begin to relax.

Next, position the tip of your tongue against the ridge of the tissue behind your upper front teeth. Keep your tongue in this position through the entire exercise, even when you're exhaling.

1.  Keeping your mouth closed, inhale gently and fully through your nose while counting to **four** in your head.

2.  Count to **seven** while holding your breath.

3.  Then, as you exhale through your mouth, slowly count to **eight** exhaling twice as long as it took for you to inhale, making a whoosh sound.

This is your first of three breaths, so repeat the 4-7-8 two more times keeping the same tempo of counts throughout.

Since many of us find trying to control our breathing awkward, pick a tempo that doesn't cause you to stress out over the counting. Speed up or slow down the count, just keep the same tempo throughout the exercise and always keep the count at 4-7-8.

Over time and with practice, slow down the tempo as you get used to inhaling and exhaling more and more deeply.

To begin with, do this subtle, but powerful, exercise twice a day. Once you have this technique under your belt, it will be a very useful tool you'll always have with you. Use this technique before reacting when anything upsetting or triggering takes place and you'll perform at a higher level. This is also a very powerful tool to help fall asleep.

# 2. CIRCLE OF EXCELLENCE

Another great technique to instantly change your mental and emotional state and prime yourself to be at your best is the Circle of Excellence technique developed by John Grinder, one of the founders of Neurolinguistic Programming (NLP). This is a great tool to create your personal High Performance state so you can create massive results for big situations or events or just to re-center yourself when you get off track.

**Step 1.** Imagine a time when you were doing something extremely well. You were confident, powerful, successful; you felt unstoppable, etc. Come up with a specific memory — make it a good one. If you've never experienced this type of situation, just imagine what it would be like.

**Step 2.** In your mind, draw a circle on the floor making it about three feet in diameter and placed about two feet in front of you. Make it large enough for you to step into. Now mentally place the memory into the circle on the floor.

**Step 3.** Actually physically step into the circle you drew and into your memory, your Circle of Excellence. Let the energy flow from your feet to your head and flood your body with the good feelings of your positive performance. Let them move through you, filling your heart, exciting your mind, lifting your spirits.

In your memory, see what you see, hear what you hear, feel what you feel, and allow the sensations to come alive as if you're in it right now. You are now literally in that positive memory reliving it and anchoring to it.

**Step 4.** As a final step, assign a color and symbol to associate with this state, e.g., a blue star or a red arrow. By attaching a color and symbol, you now anchor this High Performance state in your nervous system to call upon at any time.

Remember: Your brain doesn't know the difference between what's "real" and "imagined," so what you want to do is allow yourself to be filled with the feelings of High Performance from the memory used in the Circle of Excellence. Keep doing this until your entire being is infused from top to bottom with all the positive emotions and sensations of that High Performance memory.

You can utilize the Circle of Excellence in situations where you feel pressured, stressed, or you want to prepare your body and mind to perform at your highest level at the beginning of your day, for a meeting, negotiation, or for anything of importance where you want to be at your best. Just call upon your anchor (color and symbol) and imagine that flowing through your body creating that High Performance state.

# 3. SPINNING

This technique is amazingly fast for instantly reducing the negative impact on current or past events. The "Spin Technique" was created by Richard Bandler, co-developer of Neurolinguistic Programming (NLP). It's a powerful imaginative technique for calming heightened emotions allowing us to regulate our emotions and gain a perspective on what's happening in our lives.

What Bandler discovered in his research is that we put "spin" on our thoughts, feelings, and emotions — and they spin either clockwise or counterclockwise. Negative emotions spin in one direction, positive states and emotions spin in the opposite direction.

Interestingly, spinning a negative emotion in the opposite direction will make the negative emotion disappear. Conversely, if you spin a positive feeling even faster in its original direction, it will intensify the positive feeling.

Use these simple steps to reverse the negative emotions or thoughts connected with any situation or recurring issue:

1. Turn your focus within yourself and notice which direction the negative energy is moving: toward you (counter clockwise) or away (clockwise). Next notice what the color of the spinning energy is: red, black, blue, purple, green, etc.

2. Envision moving the spinning emotions or thoughts outside of your body and in front of yourself, then reverse its direction and color and notice the negative emotion decrease.

3. Then move the spinning energy back into your body. Make it spin faster and faster and see the color expanding into all parts of your body. Notice how your negative thoughts and emotions rapidly change until they become neutral.

As you go through this process, you may have to increase the speed of the spinning and change the color several times so that it really works for you. Take as much time as you need until the negative thoughts and emotions are neutralized.

# 4. VISUALIZATION

Another simple technique I teach clients is "Thinking from the End," a powerful technique for manifesting dreams and goals into reality. When you think from the end, you are imagining having already produced the results you desire.

In other words, you create a mental image of having already accomplished something and then you immerse yourself in the image so that you truly feel all the sensations — what you see, what you hear, what you feel — as if it's already happened.

For example: it's the middle of your day, you're highly stressed, and feel out of control. Using this visualization technique, imagine what it's like for that stress and feeling of being out of control now gone and that you're calm, at peace, and in control. Now see what you see, hear what you hear, and feel what you feel as if it's already happened — visualize this with what you're feeling for a minute or two.

Another example is to visualize your current business and personal goals that you've written down and imagining them in full Technicolor as if you've already received them. Doing that once or twice a day for a few minutes will program your subconscious mind to accelerate the acquisition of your goals.

Visualization is an extremely effective tool for programming your mind to experience more happiness, contentment, and positive benefits in all of your daily activities, as well as to expect success and achieve ever-greater results in all that you do.

# 5. GRATITUDE

Scientists are now showing that an "attitude of gratitude" has a direct and positive impact on our health and mental/emotional well being.

Dr. Robert Emmons, a professor at the University of California, Davis, has discovered what gives life meaning: gratitude. His best-selling book, *Thanks! How the New Science of Gratitude Can Make You Happier*, illustrates how people with a mindset of gratitude experience a number of benefits. They:

- Feel better about life in general
- Are more hopeful
- Are more active
- Are more passionate
- Are more resolute
- Are more intrigued and curious
- Are more elated
- Work out more
- Are sick less
- Sleep better
- Are more helpful and volunteer

Other research studies list additional benefits such as being more mentally articulate, greater resilience in difficult times, improved immune response, less stress, longer lives, enhanced family relationships, and a greater sense of spirituality.

# Cultivating a Gratitude Mindset

> ## "What you focus on expands."
> — Anonymous

In coaching my clients, two exercises I use with great results are the following:

*Create a Gratitude Journal* – A Gratitude Journal is similar to a diary, but in this case, its purpose is to list the daily experiences for which you are grateful. It's amazing how remembering these moments and events in your day can really uplift you, shifting you out of a negative state. You can acknowledge the wonderful people you know and how they add immeasurably to your life.

Just before going to bed or when you first rise in the morning, write down three things that happened that day or the previous day for which you are grateful. It can be anything that uplifted you, that made you smile, warmed your heart, a person who had a positive impact on your life, or something that will contribute toward your future happiness.

Keep a Gratitude Journal, it'll help re-program your brain so that you're focused on what's going right in your world rather than on what's wrong. The effect of keeping this journal will even positively impact your physical health.

*Seize the Moment* – Research shows that getting involved with life by volunteering, sharing with others, and having a hobby or two reaps huge benefits. And there is nothing more gratifying than knowing we've had a hand in uplifting the lives of others. That's a lot of gratitude to include in your Gratitude Journal.

University of North Carolina psychologist, Barbara Fredrickson, says, "Gratitude has the potential to change everything from its ordinary state to being a gift."

> "You can't live a perfect day without doing something for someone who will never be able to repay you."
>
> — John Wooden, Legendary UCLA Basketball Coach

# 6. LAUGHTER

Humor can be a literal lifesaver relieving pain, bringing greater happiness, and even increasing your immune system's ability to ward off illness, as well as keeping you out of your Blind Spot in difficult situations. Humor confuses the subconscious mind and stops the Blind Spot from being activated. Just as with many of the other components of High Performance Coaching, laughter can create a shift in your state of mind, creating immediate, as well as long-lasting, positive results.

## Benefits of Laughter

- Laughter reduces the output of hormones associated with stress while it increases health and wellness-enhancing hormones, which includes your immune system, and significantly mitigates the potentially devastating effects of stress. It also provides a physical and emotional release so that you feel lighter and less burdened by challenges in your life.

- Laughter is great for distracting you from negative emotions and situations. It gives you a more optimistic perspective, helping you see things as "challenges and opportunities," which makes them less intimidating and more approachable.

- Laughter is contagious and spreads all the positive benefits you experience to those around you.

# How to Use Laughter

> "Doing anything in life with the intention of having fun opens the doors to laughter."
>
> — Steven Griffith

Laughter is one of my all-time favorite stress management strategies that I use not only with clients but everyone because it's free, convenient, and has so many positive benefits. Laughter is found everywhere from books and magazines to television shows and movies. It can be shared with anyone in a multitude of situations.

Look around you. Life is hilarious in so many ways, plus, there are things about you that are humorous that can be shared with others.

# 7. HYPNOSIS

Another High Performance tool that is the foundation of the HPC 3-Step System is Hypnosis. Hypnosis is a high-impact method that is an integral part in the process of breaking through the limitations of the past and creating fast, measurable, positive performance results.

My specialized methodology is a combination of Mindfulness, Hypnosis & Meditation™ (MHM™), a proven proprietary audio conditioning program that creates a learning state in the brain that helps to re-educate, re-wire, and re-program the mind-body-brain connection. This methodology assists in removing psychological barriers (Blind Spots), immediately activates new High Performance strategies, and lets you take charge and transform your mental, emotional, physical, and financial future!

Hypnosis, referred to as hypnotherapy or hypnotic suggestion, is a trance-like state in which you have heightened focus and concentration. Also known as "sleep healing" in ancient Greece and "mind cure" in the fourteenth through mid-nineteenth centuries, it has a long history of therapeutic use.

Scientific research has shown the benefits of hypnotherapy in a number of studies. Hypnosis can help improve deep sleep and reduce pain, reduce stress and anxiety, and help remove mental blocks. In the process of hypnosis, you feel calmer and more relaxed, which allows you to bypass the critical mind's programmed resistance and you become more open to positive suggestions.

You are now well-educated about how your Blind Spots were created in early childhood and life experiences, and embedded into your subconscious mind. They were influenced by the environment and people who were consistently around you. That's why Hypnosis is so powerful when it comes to releasing and letting go of the limiting beliefs (Blind Spots) that are not true and no longer helpful to you. By utilizing hypnosis, you can directly communicate to the subconscious mind were the change needs to take place. For the fastest, long-lasting change, you have to go to the core where it started — the subconscious mind. You need to go where it was programmed and stored to begin with. Hypnosis is the fast lane to that re-programming.

Before we go any further, let's dispel the most common misconceptions about Hypnosis. For some people, going into a hypnotic trance seems weird, scary, or out of control. In fact, we experience trance states every day whether it's driving home on autopilot, surfing the web, watching a movie, daydreaming, or meditating. These forms of trance are an altered form of consciousness marked by decreased awareness — all totally normal. In Hypnosis, the difference is that you are deliberately choosing to enter this state to create the mind-body-brain connection leading to Higher Performance.

Lastly, another misconception is that while in a trance, you do not have any control over yourself or your mind. Entertainment hypnosis has had much to do with this. This is totally false. The truth is that all Hypnosis is essentially self-hypnosis in that you're either accepting or rejecting information based on your values and beliefs and what you want and don't want in life. It's a conscious choice to go into a trance in which you are completely in control. For example, if you are given a suggestion that isn't aligned with your values and beliefs, you'll reject it. That's how the subconscious mind works.

In the HPC 3-Step System, Hypnosis is a powerful tool to break through your old Blind Spots and psychological barriers and reprogram your mind in order to accelerate your results, which then allows you to let your High Performance state arise. The key is to understand that your subconscious mind does not know the difference between fantasy and reality, e.g., that's why when you wake up from a vivid dream and before you become fully awake, you're disoriented and wonder if it really happened. We know that we only use about 10 percent of our mind's capacity. When we use hypnosis, we create the opportunity to tap into the other 90 percent and rapidly make changes.

# How Can Hypnosis Help Me?

My audio conditioning system, MHM™, is designed for one thing: to be used for enhanced, accelerated performance improvement in areas of business and life that matter the most. Hypnosis has been used successfully in the following ways:

| INCREASED | DECREASED |
|---|---|
| 1. Business performance and sales | 1. Pain |
| 2. Quality of relationships | 2. Stress and anxiety |
| 3. Quality of communication | 3. Frustration |
| 4. Emotional control | 4. Fear |
| 5. Improved and deeper sleep | 5. Resistance |
| 6. Business production | 6. Distractions |
| 7. Athletic performance | 7. Negative beliefs and emotions |
| 8. Weight loss | 8. Confusion |
| 9. Resilience | 9. Overwhelm |
| 10. Focused time management | 10. Sleep difficulties |
| 11. Motivation and confidence | 11. Self-judgment |
| 12. Cognitive flexibility | 12. Mental and physical fatigue |

To most effectively receive the benefits of hypnosis, daily use is suggested. As a bonus, because you have invested your time to utilize the HPC 3-Step System, I want to help you create as much leverage for your success as possible. That's why I have included a free Hypnosis MHM™ downloadable product to help accelerate your business and personal results.

**Free Audio Bonus**
**http://www.stevengriffith.com/free-audio/**

Congratulations! You have finished the HPC 3-Step System. You've now learned what I stated in the beginning of this book: if you were not performing at your highest level, it's not your fault. Most people are being held back from their true potential because of Blind Spots that they don't even know they have.

Well, that old story is over and if you have gone through this book and followed the steps like thousands before you, you are now ready for a breakthrough — if it isn't already happening. You have everything you need and now it's a choice to uplevel your results.

Knowing is not enough, you must take action and take action now! The part of the brain that knows and the part of the brain that takes action are two different places. By making a decision to act, you instantaneously connect the two and a breakthrough will happen.

The greatest gift you have is choice. Just as you read about the Native-American story of two wolves, the good one and the evil one, you now have the conscious choice of which wolf you will feed (which emotional state you want to live in). You were designed to be the best version of you that you can be — it's the law of nature. It's time to be who you were authentically designed to be.

> "Knowing is not enough,
> We must apply.
> Willing is not enough,
> We must DO."
> — Bruce Lee

It is time for a new game of next-level results. It's time to uplevel your mindset, uplevel your skill set, uplevel your earning ability, and uplevel your impact on the world.

And finally, it is my greatest wish that you enjoy the ultimate success you deserve and that, with the help of the High Performance Coaching System, you will always perform at your highest level.

# INDEX

# ABOUT STEVEN GRIFFITH

For over 25 years, Steven has been an advocate, educator, and coach for large and small organizations, as well as one of America's most trusted coaches and advisors to CEOs, military leaders, professional and Olympic athletes, celebrities and entertainment professionals helping them perform at their very best. He is an expert in identifying the barriers (Blind Spots) in people's beliefs, behaviors, and mental and emotional patterns that keep them from achieving High Performance in their lives.

Steven is a keynote speaker and Amazon bestselling author. He is also the author of *Email Power: How to Get What You Want From Every Email You Send.* He developed the patented companion software program "EmailPower," which helps business executives and entrepreneurs increase their success when negotiating, selling, and creating online relationships with clients, customers, and colleagues. His soon to be released book is titled *How Technology is Wiring Your Kids to Fail And What to Do About It!*

He has been featured on ABC, NBC, CBS, FOX, Style and Esquire TV as a performance and communication expert. His expertise has been sought out by organizations and individuals from "Jimmy Kimmel Live," the United States Military, Citibank, Wells Fargo, the Los Angeles Police Department, USC, UCLA, The National Academy of Sports Medicine, and members of the MLB, NHL, NBA, and NFL.

## CONTACT INFORMATION

For information about individual coaching, corporate programs, and performance products, visit our web site:

www.StevenGriffith.com
310-575-0101

STEVEN GRIFFITH
HIGH PERFORMANCE COACHING